WALLFLOWERS NEED NOT APPLY

A "no bullshit" look at the world of professional screenwriting

JOHN RUSSELL

ThinkBox Publishing ▪ Vancouver, Canada

WALLFLOWERS NEED NOT APPLY

Published by

ThinkBox Publishing
a division of ThinkBox Entertainment Ltd.
1027 Davie Street, Suite 235
Vancouver, BC
Canada, V6E 4L2

All rights reserved
Copyright © 2011 by John Russell
Cover Design by Louise Adams

This book, or parts thereof, may or may not be reproduced in any form without permission from the publisher; exceptions are made for brief excerpts used in published reviews.

Library and Archives Canada Cataloguing in Publication

Russell, John E., 1960-
Wallflowers need not apply : a "no bullshit" look at
the world of professional screenwriting / John Russell.

Includes index.
ISBN 978-0-9876986-0-5

1. Motion picture authorship. I. Title.

PN1996.R87 2011 808.2'3 C2011-905600-3

Books written by John Russell can be obtained either through the Publisher's official website:

www.thinkboxpublishing.com

or through select online book retailers

For L, M & S

Contents

Begin With A Beginning	9
I'm Going To Be In Deep Shit	11
Another Year Gone	14
Top Questions	16
The Title Gets Worked In	20
I Want A Check, Please!	23
Too Many Readers	26
Forward Thinking	28
Simplify	30
Get Real	33
Take The Pain!	35
It's All In The Timing	37
Literary Chicken & Egg	40
Producers Are People, Too	42
Get After It	44
Go Produce Yourself!	46
Flash Meet Pan?	51
Your Second Marriage	53
Out Of The Comfort Zone	55
The Authentic Writer	58
Writers Fright	61
You Know What?	64
This Is Not Novel Work	67
Excuses, Excuses…?	70
On The Nose	72
Flame Free Bridges	74
Enter The Variables	77
Take It Or Leave It	80
What A Character	83
"Original" Thought	86
Got Guts?	88
Why Do You Do It?	91

Hello, It's Me	93
Genre Specific	95
Trend + Luck = Opportunity	97
Show Me Yours	99
Zip It!	101
ABC's	105
Why/What?	109
Could've Had a V-8	110
Parenthetical Madness	113
Luck Off	116
Blocky Description	119
Rub Out The Nub	122
From Scratch	124
Wake Up	126
ComedyQuest	128
Live It	130
Market Wise	134
You're Gonna Make It	138
Market Wise-Up	142
Autobio-Dwell	145
Voice	148
Proper Groupings	151
No Time Like The Present	155
Screenwriting Biz 101	157
A Closer Look At Book Rights	160
Network!!!	163
Psst, Buddy, Wanna Buy An Idea?	166
The Real Writing Begins	168
Floating Scripts	172
Voices Of Screenplays Future	174
Consultations	177
Screenwriting Contests: Yes or No?	179
What If?	181
And The Protagonist Is?	183
To Montage, Or Not To Montage	185

Thick Skin	187
It's A Brevity Thing, Man	190
Write Short	193
Freewheeling Into Nothingness	195
Yo, Grammar Nerds	197
There's No Denying It	199
End At The Ending	201
Index	204
About the Author	210

Wallflowers Need Not Apply

"Be regular and orderly in your life, so that you may be violent and original in your work."
									-- Gustave Flaubert

Introduction

Begin With A Beginning

This book contains, in no particular order, an assortment of chapters dealing with navigating the business, and craft, of screenwriting. I've been a professional writer for nearly 20 years. I am not a 'superstar' screenwriter by any means, but I do get paid for my work. I offer this collection of 'working writer' advice in hopes that it will assist new screenwriters as well as others who have not yet secured paid writing deals.

John Russell is not my real name. I wrote this under a pen name for the simple fact that I want to continue writing screenplays. "Hollywood" has a way of unofficially disowning those who write books that provide professional advice to novices. Not a good enough reason for you? Okay, I want you to think hard about your favorite "book-writing-screenplay-experts" and all the movies they've had hit the theaters in recent years. Go ahead and check Imdb, I'll wait. Couldn't find too many, could you? Now you know why I use a pseudonym.

If you're the type of person who needs to be handled with kid gloves as you traverse the world of screenwriting, you have picked up the wrong book. I'm not about gentle persuasion or coddling.

I can be rather blunt, a little crass, and like any decent coach I hammer certain important points home by repeating them often, but I always have the end goal for you in mind - to become a professional writer.

You could call this a niche screenwriting book, and I would have no qualms with that. Mass appeal is not the name of the game for this tome. I am not about handing out 'rose-colored glasses' guidance. But if you do still read this book cover-to-cover, even after I've given you a no-nonsense disclaimer, you're on the proper track to possibly becoming a paid writer.

Most of all, if you're going to have at least a chance at this profession, you'll need to come out of the screenwriting gate with a ton of natural creative talent. You'll also need to possess a willingness to listen, learn, and be disciplined in your writing regimen. This is a VERY competitive business -- as competitive as making it in professional sports.

Toughen up as quickly as you can. And never take your eye off the goal of getting your work optioned, sold, and produced. Never.

Chapter 1

I'm Going To Be In Deep Shit

I had the pleasure of being on a panel at a small yet highly regarded film festival in California a while back. I'm not paid to be on panels, I just simply enjoy doing them. I wasn't completely sure how the panel would work, especially since the organizers placed me on a panel with a famous documentary filmmaker.

A famous documentary filmmaker…and me - bizarre.

Well, it worked out.

You know, storytelling is storytelling, no matter the vehicle you choose or use (narrative or documentary) to accomplish your story telling task.

And as it happens after such panels, I'm approached (in person or through email) by some of the fine folks who took the time out of their busy lives to pay attention to what I have to say. The majority of these people are looking for an edge, maybe some kernel of inside information that I can impart so that they can get a jump on the competition and flourish in their new-chosen screenwriting venture.

Wallflowers Need Not Apply

I've had a few writer successes in my career. Any bit of success I've carved out for myself never came from any "secret" that I could remember.

Okay, check that.

Shit, I probably shouldn't do this...

It'll go against the confidential regulations and conventions of all screenwriters who have actually made money performing their craft. I may be banned from the secret screenwriters society (so covert that I can't even mention the name of the organization).

Here it is. Here's the "secret" to obtaining success. Oh, man, I'm gonna be in deep shit now with the others in the group.

The secret is...

Write, write, and fucking WRITE some more! And that does not mean writing one (singular) screenplay over and over again, ace. Write several different spec screenplays. That's the "secret." Get the words out of your head, through your fingers, and onto the page. Rinse, wash and repeat -- and repeat again, and again, and again.

And it's reality check time, people -- Having natural talent for story telling is a kinda-sorta good thing to possess, too.

And as you complete screenplay after screenplay, begin to network with as many industry people as you can. They don't have to be top tier folks, just people with similar career passions. You can find networking opportunities at writers conferences, film festivals, taking trips to LA or NYC, and getting yourself out there pretty much any (legal or otherwise) way you can. To me, being adept at networking is almost as important as being a gifted writer. But being a good writer should come first. The screenwriting chicken starts with a "good writer/storyteller" egg.

The "secret" is exposed.

Tell my wife that I love her...

Chapter 2

Another Year Gone

It's happened to all of us. You're bent out of shape because some life goal isn't happening quicker than you'd expect, and you have an elder member of your family kindly telling you to relax. You know the old, "Good things come to those who wait," line? Here's what you do.

Don't listen to them.

They're not talking about becoming a screenwriter.

Do you hear that ticking sound coming from your laptop? That's the Movie Magic/Final Draft doomsday clock winding down.

Writing screenplays is more of a craft than an art, so along with your excellent story telling sense (you better have it), and your creative flare (also a prerequisite); you need to get your screenwriting ass in your screenwriting chair and get after it. Now! Learning a craft takes time.

Write four or five shitty screenplays to get the words out of your system. Hell, the 2nd or 3rd one may even be good enough to approach Producers with. But getting those first horrible words out of your head and onto three-holed punched paper will open you up for the better words and improved screenplay execution to follow.

You'll soon find your writer's voice (very important), and discover that, yeah you can actually place your personality into your screenwriting. Does this last sentence sound like a 'no shit' to you? Most new screenwriters don't have a clue as to how to place their personality into their work. Writing those four or five crappy screenplays will help you get beyond that point.

You wouldn't expect a carpenter to build the most perfect example of woodworking art the first time out of the gate, would you? Carpentry is a craft – screenwriting is a craft. It takes time to perfect your skill. But that means you need to start now – don't wait.

And again, I bring this up because of the MANY times I've been approached by new screenwriters (an inordinate amount recently) who expect that their first and only screenplay will launch their careers. The odds are that it won't. Unofficially, based on my experiences with other professional writers, it'll take writing about 5 or more screenplays before you'll even make any inroads into the professional world of writing (probably more). I'm sure there are writers who have done it much quicker, but that's not the norm.

No time to waste, people. Build those screenplays!

Chapter 3

Top Questions

A writing friend of mine had a blog for a time, and tracked the search engine results that drove traffic to her website. Her readers (mostly Newbie writers) found her blog by using the same 4 Internet searches/questions time after time. Here they are, along with a brief answer from me to those same searches/questions:

"Odds of selling my screenplay?"

Answer: Shitty.

Equate it to winning the lottery. But to even have a chance you have to put in hours and hours of writing time to get yourself in the running. Screenwriting isn't easy – at all. Just because you've watched a whole bunch of movies, doesn't mean that you can write one. But here's the flip side of this statement; your spec may not sell, but your excellent writing may get you an assignment down the line. So, if you're truly interested in screenwriting, you must keep writing. And that does not mean writing the exact same screenplay over and over again.

"Screenwriter's salary?"

Answer: The WGA has minimums placed on what you'll be paid for screen/television/web writing. You can find those dollar amounts at www.wga.org.

But if you're not a WGA member, you could literally "sell" your screenplay for nothing, or $1,000,000 or more if someone's willing to pay that amount for it. Generally speaking, in the Hollywood movie game, the screenwriter(s) usually gets 3% of the production budget -- if the writer is established and has a history of success. Lately though even the seasoned vets are making WGA minimums up front with the promise of a larger back end deal. If you're just starting out you'll (normally) be looking at the lower end of the money scale. And I mean the lowest end. What you'll probably find is that the "starting pay" for most non-WGA screenwriters working with equally new Producers is closer to $0.

And actually, no one really "sells" screenplays. They option the property to a Producer in hopes the Producer raises the production budget money to actually make the film. The real money comes when the movie goes into production in most cases.

"Page to minute ratio?"

Answer: One minute per page is the average. So the 120-page screenplay you've completed should be 2 hours long. However (!) that's for a fairly clutter free page. If you're a novelistic screenwriter, placing every little fricking detail and action into your work, having huge heaping lumps of text on the page, etc., that one minute per page scenario can get tossed to the wayside in a heartbeat. I've read 120-page specs that, if filmed, would be 4-hour long movies. The writer crammed that much shit onto their pages. And realistically, the novelistic screenplays would probably never even get past a professional Reader/Producer. Text heavy pages will get you tossed pretty quickly.

"Price of book rights?"

Answer: If it's a book from the New York Times Best Seller list, it'll cost you a LOT of money. But there's really no set fee for purchasing film rights for a book. With the experiences I've had, $5,000 was a low-end figure for a 1-year option. But that's fairly low end. That money buys you one year to write the screenplay and put together the money/talent to make the movie. Most times, that process takes a bit longer so you'll have to renegotiate every year, or set up a clause in the initial deal that will allow you to "buy" the rights year after year for a set number of years.

And remember, the primary book/film rights deal is most times taken care of as part of the initial publishing deal with the book's author. So sometimes you'll actually be dealing with an entirely different owner (other than the original book publisher) to get the rights secured. One bit of advice if you're going after a best seller is to get a good entertainment attorney on your side from the start. You'll need the expertise in your corner.

Now, if it's a smaller or self-published book, you may have a shot at approaching and showing the rights owner your passion for the project. That may be enough to get them to make a "free" up front/paid on the back end deal with you. The problem with the smaller books is that if it doesn't have an audience (or a star actor interested in being in the movie version) your chances of selling it up the ladder to a Producer who can actually get the film produced are pretty slim. It's all about money/popularity at that point. And you know what, get an entertainment attorney involved either way, it may save you some heartache and money.

Chapter 4

The Title Gets Worked In

Should you attend screenwriting conferences?

Quite a few of the well-known (well-worn?) screenwriting "experts" who regularly make the conference rounds have successfully produced books, DVDs, and webcasts covering their know-how. You could buy up all this "expert" material and dive in hoping to set out on a screenwriting career. So, is it a must to attend screenwriting conferences? No.

However – there are three very important words that come to mind when I think about screenwriting conferences…

Networking – Networking - Networking.

Of course you can absorb an expert's advice while watching them on DVD in the comfort of your own home, or by reading their books. But nothing compares to actually being surrounded by your peers as you soak in all that is screenwriting. And often times there are those magical moments when a working professional (not just some screenwriting expert who's never had a credit) new to the conference circuit shows up to put their unique 'not the usual bullshit' spin on useful information.

Why watch an expert on DVD when you could be having a beer with him/her after the conference sessions? Some screenwriting conferences are that intimate. This type of face-to-face camaraderie happens all the time. You can't really get that from a webcast.

Attending a conference can be a very fruitful place to make connections. Those new networking connections can sometimes last a lifetime. You'll be among peers of varying ranges of screenwriting competency. At the conferences where I've been a panelist, most times, the attendees seem to establish a one-for-all, all-for-one type of attitude, sharing what they've learned, and working as a big team to kick-start each other's careers. The competitive nature of show business will come later, but while at the conference, they're learning their craft and sharing amongst each other.

Show business is definitely an industry of relationships. You've probably heard that a million times, but it's so very true, and worth repeating. If you're not getting yourself out into the screenwriting world, your chances of ever making it will be greatly diminished. My unofficial credo for all new screenwriters is this: "Wallflowers need not apply." If you are a bit shy, get over it as quickly as you can, because you're doing a disservice to any shot you may have at being a successful screenwriter.

Bottom line - You have to know what you're doing as a screenwriter, but it's also quite important to know the right people, as well. Those networking connections have to start somewhere, especially if you're not living in LA or NYC.

Wallflowers Need Not Apply

Attending a conference could be a good way for you to become and stay connected.

Chapter 5

I Want A Check, Please!

I'm writing this under the assumption that you're striving to be a professional screenwriter. If you're not, you can stop reading. There's absolutely nothing wrong with hobbies. Hey, they break up the monotony of life, right? My hobby is cooking. I'm experimenting with lemon chicken tonight.

You want a shot at actually making some money in this business?

You MUST have the ability to create & write a lot of material, and the capability to juggle several projects at once. Either finished writing projects that you're currently marketing, or writing-in-progress projects you want to have on the market soon. You need "irons in the coals."

Having one fantastic screenplay is an incredible achievement, but it's most likely not going to get you far if you can't back it up. I know, I know. You hear about the one-hit-wonders who sold a (singular) screenplay for a million bucks and they haven't done anything since. I bet if you dig a little deeper, you'd discover that those 1-screenplay-wonders have several completed screenplays that never saw the light of day. I'd bet that they had to crank out the material and put in a few years time, meeting people, making themselves known, before they acquired that one-hit-wonder status.

The reason I bring this up is because through my travels and my discussions with new screenwriters (something I do almost daily), I hear the same thing time and time again. "I want to make this screenplay perfect before sending it out and writing anything else."

That's an admirable goal – and you should always be working toward your definition of perfection, but you may want to rethink taking a few years to perfect that one screenplay. You may want to train yourself to hammer out the words. The more words you have travel through your fingertips and into your computer (or pen to paper) the better your chances of getting the shitty words out of your system. The sooner this happens you may discover that you have the ability to come up with almost the right words the first time out of the gate (i.e. story lines, structure, dialogue et al).

The realities of the film business are that you have to have the gift to, for a lack of a better term, crank out the material. That does not connote "hacking" your way through your screenplays. It means writing to the top of your ability, consistently, and quickly.

That "quickly" part will come into play when you are hired on assignment, something you should definitely be pushing for. That's where the bread & butter screenwriting money is.

Your capacity to have several "irons in the coals" is your possible ticket to a professional screenwriting career. And I don't know about you, but I want to keep working, so honing my ability to constantly come up with marketable material is something I work for – always.

Chapter 6

Too Many Readers

You've completed a few drafts of your latest screenplay and you're now ready for others to take a look at your work before approaching Producers.

Who do you have read your screenplay?

Someone you can trust, right? Someone who will give you a professional even handed read, without getting too 'personal.'

I only have a few people read my first drafts, one of them being my agent. I don't want a lot of opinions, just focused ones.

Focused, how?

I try to get three to five people of varying degrees of screenwriting/filmmaking competency (both male and female) to give their honest opinions. I don't need coddling. In fact, I would rather have someone completely take the piece apart bit by bit, than have them say, 'That was nice.' I know that 'nice' will never cut it.

So having your Mom read your screenplay probably isn't going to help you much – unless your Mom is Tina Fey.

I purposefully ask my trusted readers about portions of the screenplay that I know I'm having trouble with. I want to make sure all bases are covered whenever possible.

Why only a few readers?

I don't want hordes of people reading the work at this point because their opinions will begin canceling each other out. Think 'too many cooks.' You had to trust your gut when you began the difficult process of writing the screenplay in the first place. For me it's best to go with that gut instinct and a few trusted readers to get me to the point where I believe the screenplay should meet the world.

Now get those initial reads – and move on to the real writing.

The rewriting!

Chapter 7

Forward Thinking

I have daily doubts about my writing ability. If the work is professional enough, if the story elements will grab an audience, if the characters are fleshed out and real. And I wonder if I can pay the bills with what I've created. Hell, I'm having doubts about this chapter.

But there's also an unseen "something" that keeps driving me forward. Gladly the forward driving influence is stronger than that 'what in the hell am I doing, and why is there a talking dung beetle in my screenplay?' force.

What drives me (or any writer) forward? I'm not completely sure. And, really, why analyze it – I tend to write all the time. I don't necessarily enjoy writing, but for whatever reason I can gather the gumption to place my ass in the seat and do what I have to do.

Hopefully your self-doubt isn't completely handcuffing you as a writer. If you're discovering that you can't make your writing perfect the first time in a first draft and you stop the project completely – yeah – that can be a problem. It's good to be a perfectionist in screenwriting, but only after you get a first draft on paper. Otherwise perfectionism can really fuck with your writers' head.

When I get to those points in my first drafts where I'm not sure what to do, I tend to put 'place holders' in my screenplays and continue toward Fade Out. Of course, I'll have to return to the 'place holders' at some point or another to complete the job. When I do revisit the 'place holders' my mind is more open to ideas and I'm not so flummoxed that I can't figure out what to write. I'll literally write a slug line and under that "Something funny happens here," or ""Dramatic turn," etc. And then I keep moving toward Fade Out.

Of course I can always refer back to my outline to assist me along the way.

You are outlining, right?

If you're continuously getting stumped on where to go next in your screenplay, the lack of an outline (a map) is probably the root cause of your troubles. You have to know where you're eventually going, even if you take side trips from time to time.

Sometimes when you're at a writers' cul-de-sac, though, you have to simply muscle your way through. Put anything down on paper and move forward.

Always move forward.

Chapter 8

Simplify

Counter-intuitive advice to follow: Simplify your fricking spec screenplays, people.

One of the problems I see with some brand new writers is that they believe they have to go way overboard in outdoing what Hollywood has already done. That's an admirable goal, but the fact is, most spec screenplays don't have a chance in hell of ever selling. New screenwriters have a way of overwriting, and out thinking themselves from the chance of getting noticed.

I'm not advocating having 'nothing happen' in your screenplays. Make sure you have a compelling story, just simplify your next draft, and see what happens. You may be surprised. Mies Van Der Rohe was right, less can be more.

If you have a unique writing style, and a strong writer's voice, you may have a chance at this. And the best way to showcase that skill and talent is to write a simple, and straightforward, screenplay.

I've read many, many screenplays and, unfortunately, the vast majority of them are shitty (some of mine included). Why complicate matters by creating a contrived, 'too complex,' and hard to follow story line, when you can try to come up with a simple idea that's turned slightly on its head? That 'turning it on its head' is the freshness you bring to the table.

Selling/optioning a spec script is a bit of a lottery shot – but you already know that, right? Getting Producers/Executives to notice your writing style is a much more solid approach to trying for some sort of (paid) writing career. The Producer/Executives may have all sorts of complicated stories they want to produce already in their stables. Show them your unique writer's voice and maybe you'll be the person they hire to write their screenplay. The best way to exhibit that voice is to keep them mesmerized with your "simplicity."

Show the people who are making decisions that you can write excellent descriptions and compelling dialogue, and yeah, maybe even surprise them a bit with how you approach your story. Just try to not over complicate things. Write economically, but descriptively.

I know this may sound like crazy-talk advice to some of you, but I think if you allow what I'm saying to sink in, you'll see that it may be worth your time to consider.

Strive to create excellent, well crafted (by not overwriting), screenplays. Use the least and 'bestest' words possible for your descriptions. Show it; don't say it all through dialogue. Create real characters and snappy dialogue - just not overtly expositional dialogue. That kind of work has a way of getting you noticed.

Wallflowers Need Not Apply

It doesn't guarantee a sale or even an assignment, but at least you'll have a chance.

By 'simplifying,' and putting down on paper just what needs to be there, you'll become a better screenwriter.

Chapter 9

Get Real

Topic: Ethereal fantasy bullshit screenplays.

Just stop writing them. Please. No one cares that you created "characters like you've never seen before from the planet Whatisthisbullshit."

I'll let you in on a little fiction-writing secret…

If your fantasy story and your characters are 'like nothing that has ever been done before,' your story will suck. Fantasy works best when anchored in some sort of reality we can, well, relate to. Remember the first Star Wars movie? It's a very basic 'save the princess' type film with World War I dogfights thrown in. "But what about Avatar, that's like nothing I've ever watched?"

Okay, you mean you've never heard of the story of Pocahontas and John Smith? We've seen the stories before – and yet – had not seen special effects like that. That's the difference.

Fantasy, at least for me, works best when it's based in reality but turned a little on its head. It has to have some sort of fresh twist

Wallflowers Need Not Apply

tossed in to make it interesting.

"But I'm creating whole new worlds that have never been seen before."

Pffft…Sell it down the line, ace, because you're going to have one hell of a time making a deal on your 'nothing like anything else' screenplay. What makes fantasy scarier, more emotional, more comical, more exciting, is when we relate to what's happening on screen. We can see our own selves in the story. Basing fantasy in reality plays those oh-so twisted mind games with us…

And we'll pay to see that.

Chapter 10

Take The Pain!

Here's a challenge for you –

Find an acquaintance that believes you to be the biggest dreamer/time waster for following this screenwriting fantasy of yours and get them to read your latest work from cover-to-cover. For me, that would be my wife. Hi, honey…

And after they complete the read, your second challenge, if you choose to accept it, is to sit and listen to their 'notes' without rebuttal. Bup-bup-bup. You'll have to keep your mouth shut and listen to every 'note' they have.

Now why would you want to do such a thing?

Well, because this is an excellent way to make your screenplays stronger through subsequent rewrites, and it's also a fantastic way to get real world experience without the possibility of ruining a chance at making a sale to an actual Hollywood Producer/Executive. Use the semi-adversarial relationship with your acquaintance to stand-in for the dealings you'll (hopefully) have with the real life Producer/Executives you encounter.

Wallflowers Need Not Apply

But why would you even attempt something like this? Because coercing someone who is admittedly not your biggest advocate into reading your work is probably easier than getting a real Producer/Executive to read your stuff.

Assuming you can talk this 'acquaintance' into doing this favor for you, how non-judgmental do you think their notes will be? But, if you can wow this known semi-antagonist with your spectacular writing - maybe, just maybe, you have a shot at impressing some Producer/Executive in Hollywood.

Maybe…

And really, you won't have anything to worry about if/when you finally do get your work into the Hollywood Producer/Executive's hands because they're all so very nice.

Brooohahahaha!

Chapter 11

It's All In The Timing

There are so many schools of thought on the topic of timing and screenplay structure.

For me, here's a simplistic 'formula' that most good movies follow (besides having killer story lines, great acting, and fantastic direction). It's a pacing issue that I've noticed in the films I enjoy and that have the most emotional impact on me. I'm not going to give you specific film examples. You'll have to trust yourself to know it when you see it. It's a dangerous assumption I know.

Simply sit with your favorite movie on DVD and when important story points are revealed, or the character is thrown in a new direction, check the DVD timer (making sure you noted the actual start time, that is). You'll soon discover that these moments occur in the areas of (these are ish's people) minute/page 10, 15, 30, 45, 60, 75, and 90. This is based on any film of 100 or more minutes, and adjusted down slightly for shorter films. I also do this timing thing while in the theater with my silenced cell phone clock. My wife refuses to go to the movies with me anymore because I'm always saying, "Look! The midpoint was at the 59 minute mark." Yeah, I'm that guy...

Again, very simplistically stated, we should know your protagonist and what they're first desires are by page 10. Page 15 is a time when something important pushes the protagonist forward. By page 30 the story should be well underway. Page 45 is another shove for the protagonist. Page 60 everything is turned on its head for your main character – and the direction of the film most times changes dramatically. Page 75 is another goodly smack to the story. Page 90 you should begin rocketing to the satisfying ending.

And when I see a film that's somehow "off," I'll notice that the number count from above is not in play. That's when my ass starts hurting from being in the seat too long. The film is out of whack and not balanced. You know what I'm talking about. Okay here's an older example of this. Peter Jackson's King Kong missed the timing mark for me. His page 30 happened near the 60-minute mark. I knew I was in for an ass-burner that day – and I was. The film was way too long and out of step. Overall it was okay, but not great. When these things happen I usually note the other audience members' reactions, too. Guess what? There's usually a lot of squirming in the seats – looking at the person next to them with a 'what gives' expression, that sort of thing. Audiences know when the timing is off.

As I read more and more un-produced screenplays I see this same scenario play out time and time again. Check that, I see it NOT playing out in the majority of the Newbie's screenplays. What I see there is really nothing happening at all until after page 30. I don't know why that is, it just is. If you're not rocketing out of the gate in the first ten pages, grabbing your reader, and keeping a hold of them until Fade Out, you're going to have a tough time with this profession. That page count scenario from above can help you keep your reader/audience's attention.

Read over your current drafts to see if your screenplay is even close to the 10, 15, 30, 45, 60, 75, 90-page number 'important shit happening' count. If it's not, try thinking of ways to get it closer to that count. You may be surprised to find that you'll have a more focused, cohesive, and interesting screenplay in your hands.

Chapter 12

Literary Chicken & Egg

"I've written a novel and now I want to adapt it into a screenplay. I know that many movies are made from books. I've heard that writing the novel first is a better way to sell my idea to a film Producer. Do you agree?"

Not completely.

Outside of the usual 'is this a genre I work in' question, here are a few other things that may be asked by any Producer you approach –

Has your book been financially successful?

How many copies of the book have been sold?

Is it on a best sellers list? Which ones?

Is it a popular book (outside of sales, is it often spoken of by the general public)?

Is it critically acclaimed (by critically acclaimed sources)?

Generally speaking, just because it's in book format doesn't automatically make it better fuel for the movie making machine. Like many other businesspeople, a Producer wants to efficiently invest their time, energy and money into a proven entity. Most people in this business are a bit 'risk averse' and 'risk takers' all rolled into one.

The prevailing thought process is something along these lines -- the movie business, as a whole, is uncertain at best, so why exacerbate that risk with unknowns?

And if you do approach a Producer with your book idea, make sure your screenplay is already written, especially if your book doesn't have a financial track record. The reason is this -- you'll be going after two major "asks" from the Producer at that point. One - for the Producer to take on an unknown property, and B - you'll be asking them to pony up the dough to hire someone to write the screenplay for them (if you're not performing that task), or to wait you out while you complete that writing process, too.

Chapter 13

Producers Are People, Too

I was a panelist at big southern California film festival for a few years running and I met so many writers who were afraid to approach the Producers in attendance. It was confounding to me. And the Producers/Executives were right in front of them – there for the taking/talking/pitching/or whatevering.

It's time to remove the mystique from the apparently lofty Hollywood Producer. What are you afraid of? Producers are simply regular people trying to earn a living (and if they're any good at their job, a pretty decent living). Their task is to find the most gripping screenplays/stories they can so they can possibly produce a money making film in the future.

Your job is to provide them with the material they desire so they can complete their jobs. Your task is also to be able to actually approach and speak with said Producer in order to let them know you're a screenwriter with product to be read.

It's pretty fricking simple stuff, really.

If you approach your writing career in a more 'blue-collar' way, endlessly writing and creating excellent material, the chances of you providing one of these Producers with what they desire will rise incrementally.

And if you do finally shake the nerves to go after Producers with your material here's what you'll soon learn…

The majority of Producers work in tiny offices on back lots, or above storefronts on Wilshire Blvd., or the like. You'll discover that Producers usually don't have several layers of minions serving below them. A lot of times you'll find that the offices have only 2 or 3 people in them. So if you ever get the nerve to actually 'phone pitch' a Producer, the odds are pretty good that the person answering the phone is only a few feet, and a flimsy wall, away from the Producer him/herself.

You want to try and make deals in Hollywood, right? You need to be talking to the people who actually make those deals happen – Producers. Not agents, not managers – but Producers. Having an agent and/or a manager is a great thing, but it's not an end all, "I can stop and let my rep do the heavy lifting," proposition. You still have to push your own career forward.

Lose the Producer mystique and start making contacts.

Chapter 14

Get After It

"I've got a new credo/motto for shy 'closeted screenwriters.' How do you expect to write about characters if you don't go out and meet some?" – J. Russell's writer friend Jon

I like Jon's approach – it's no bullshit, and man does he have a point.

Off topic/On topic here for a moment…

I know where Jon is coming from because I've been to film festivals and screenwriting conferences where some, not all, of the attendees are very reticent about approaching other writers/producers/muckety-mucks. You'll usually find these non-starters standing near a corner of the room, looking at their shoes, sipping from overpriced bottles of sparkling water – and basically ignoring everyone.

Come on, folks, you got yourself to the event why not make the most of it. Introduce yourself, meet some people in-the-know, and pick their brains. They're there for the asking. Back on topic -- Maybe I'm wrong, but I'd guess that if these fearful writers are not even approaching people in the same business to discuss their interests, they probably aren't researching their screenplay characters by going out and meeting the real people who are living the actual lives of their characters.

Writing about SWAT teams? Go out and ask a local SWAT team if you can tag along for one of their training sessions. Maybe your character is a furniture storeowner? Find one in your area and take them out for a drink, see if you can observe them at work. Your imagination will be charged ten-fold because you'll be pulling from actual occurrences you've observed through your research. How about that sketchy dude talking to himself at the mall? Yeah, well…you get the idea.

When I see people standing in the corner of the room, looking at their shoes, etc., I head over and introduce myself, and talk them up. Yeah, I know I'm an enabler at that point, but what the hell. I usually end up in some great conversations. But, come on, wall huggers, step out of that shell. Introduce yourself to the writing world, and to the world at large. You want a shot at this screenwriting thing, right?

What are you waiting for? Live a life outside of your writer's hovel. Your work will be much more interesting for your efforts.

Chapter 15

Go Produce Yourself!

I'm actually a little amazed that so many new writers don't realize what a Producer does.

So here's the answer --- They do whatever it takes to get a film produced and distributed. Sure, this simple answer is a bit all encompassing, but that's really the answer.

Now specifically what does a Producer do?

Wait -- hold on a minute.

I want to state that prior to becoming your own Producer, or a Producer for someone else's screenplay, you should know in advance that it's not an easy task. Producing takes a lot of time, energy, and yes, access to money (or access to access to money). Unfortunately, even having all of these components in place doesn't guarantee success. But people produce films all the time, so...

Okay – Here are a few (not all), simply stated, tasks a Producer performs to see their productions through to completion.

Producers find screenplays they believe will become financially successful films. It's not "Show Art." This is business, plain and simple. A Producer has to find the property that they believe will put the most butts in the seats. They negotiate the fees they'll pay for the use/ownership of said screenplay. The Producer can also work to get you (the original writer) or another writer to rewrite the screenplay to their exact specifications.

Producers most times locate financial partners to share the risk of movie making. Low-end Hollywood productions are coming in at about $15 million (average is more like $50 million+) so finding someone to share the risk can be a smart business move. This is why you see so many Production Company names all linked together while those opening credits are rolling at your local theater ("SoandSo Productions, in conjunction with, BlahBlah Pictures, in association with Whatchamacallit Studios, Present --").

Sometimes when Producers run these development deals up the ladder to a larger entity (Production Company/Studio) seeking financial partners, the larger entity will (possibly) buy out the smaller company and then go on to make the film in their own way.

Producers work distribution deals before the cameras even begin to roll. On most Indie filmmaking ventures the hope is to get distribution before the cameras roll, but more often than not, the deals will be made once the film is complete. The Indie world can be a risky place to work in as well. And just because a budget is smaller, doesn't necessarily mean that the Producer's job is any easier. It's not.

Wallflowers Need Not Apply

Producers find the talent to actually make the film happen. They locate Directors, Actors, Cinematographers, Set Designers, etc. They work on finding locations to film, obtaining permits, etc. And they negotiate the fees they are going to pay for each of these elements in the filmmaking process. They need to learn the rules and regulations of all the union employees they'll have in their charge. Or hire someone who does know.

Producers make sure the production of the film is running smoothly. In a lot of cases the Producer (s) doesn't even need to be on set – especially if they hired the right people to get the film made in the first place.

Producers make sure the production and ultimately the post-production is staying on budget and on time. Again, if they hired the right people to begin with, this job will hopefully be without major headaches (major ones, anyway…).

These are just a few of the main Producer jobs for a film production.

Okay, so you're a "No-Name-Screenwriter" in, let's say, Tiny Town, Indiana, how do you begin becoming your own Producer?

It starts with an excellent screenplay – and money. I know this harkens back to the old Steve Martin joke, "I can tell you how to become a millionaire. First get a million dollars."

Money talks, folks. If you haven't figured this out already, the majority of Producers in the Hollywood system are from money to begin with. So how do you get money people's attention?

Here's how -- Through your passion for your project, and your talent for writing an excellent screenplay.

You must believe in your project. You must exude confidence that your screenplay will become a profit making film. And you have to get yourself in front of money people, or people who have access to money people. Even if you attract a small portion of the funds for the final budget for your film, you could then approach a known Production Company in LA or NYC and see if they would like to partner with you.

Money talks.

And before you say, "Oh, so it's not about talent, it's about how much money you have," know this. It will be your talent for writing an incredible screenplay and your passion for your project that will attract that money.

The people who invest in film are not always "Movie People." They're financiers, doctors, lawyers, bankers, etc. Look into how the Coen Brothers financed their film *Blood Simple*. (Hint: Dentists - lots and lots of Dentists)

Make sure to check all the FTC rules and regulations before you Produce your own films and begin approaching financial backers. Research as to how to write up a business plan ("package") for your film production - there are actually software programs available out there that will guide you through this process.

Producing is not easy, and it's not for the weak-of-heart, but it can be done – it's done on a daily basis.

You believe in your work. You're very passionate about your story, and confident of your ability to write an excellent screenplay, right? Then what are you waiting for?

Chapter 16

Flash Meet Pan?

I've had a lot of recent correspondences with writers who have written one, maybe two screenplays and expect things to happen for them. While I wish them the very best as they endeavor to be 'Hollywood trend buckers' (try saying that 10 times as fast as you can), the general reality is that it'll take writing several screenplays and more than a few years for you to at least get a toe-hold in the business. And that's if you're living in LA or NYC, or travel there for meetings on a regular basis.

Successful writers simply don't write one or two screenplays and stop to market those few, and only those few screenplays (okay, Affleck and Damon did, but that's a whole other story). True screenwriters are always creating, even on top of the assignments they may possibly be hired to write. It's what they do, and who they are. You can't shut it off.

Writers write.

I'd venture to guess that for every screenplay an A-List screenwriter has had produced there are at least 5 of their completed screenplays, probably more, that will never see the

Wallflowers Need Not Apply

light of day.

If you plan on making a dent in the professional screenwriting world, you can't take your journey lightly. Have fun with it, sure, but this is serious business. I know you probably have a regular day gig and a family that take up your precious time, but so did the majority of the current A-List screenwriters when they were coming up through the ranks. You have to creatively manage your time so that you can give yourself the shot that you deserve.

Yes, pretty much anyone can write a screenplay, but can they be financially successful at it? It is a business. Do we all possess the talent to convey a compelling story with fantastic visual imagery and snappy dialogue? You're entering a very competitive world where there are many talented folks attempting to do exactly the same as you. Screenwriting doesn't usually turn out to be a hobby that pays off (there go those 'trend buckers' again).

I'm not writing this as a way of saying you'll never make it. I'm writing to kick you all in the ass so that you get after your careers. Learn the craft, which can take writing several completed screenplays to master. Then keep creating - and write, write, and write some more.

It's really the only tried and true way of at least having a shot at a screenwriting career.

Writers write.

Chapter 17

Your Second Marriage

Remember the old saying, "Never go into business with a member of your own family?" Writing collaborations are like that, too.

Whether it'll be an excellent partnership or not actually depends on who the partners are. If you get along swimmingly, it can seemingly work out quite well. If you're in a contentious battle of the wills to even get your ideas onto the page? Not so much – seemingly.

Why seemingly?

Well, because what may seem like a pain in the ass, and a daily chore to get your words on paper, could actually be something quite special. That battle of the wills, a lot of the time, is what will make your screenplay better. You and your writing partner will challenge one another to up each other's screenwriting game. That can be a great thing for your final product.

Conversely, if everything is just flowing along great – no problems – and you actually hear little songbirds chirping as

Wallflowers Need Not Apply

you write in tandem under lush fruit laden trees, my guess is that your stuff is probably going to suck. That's my cynical take on it, anyway. I could be wrong. Most times, at least for me, when things are 'easy' they're usually shitty, too.

Writing teams have double the problems – double the attitude – and double the family/personal problems that seep into their daily writing regime.

But they can also have two times the creativity. You have an instant sounding board. And in a good writing team, you have a partner who is willing to put it all on the line to make sure the screenplay is the best it can possibly be.

Here's the monetary downside…

If you can get past all the relationship bullshit to complete a screenwriting masterpiece – you have to share the fucking paycheck when you make the deal.

Chapter 18

Out Of The Comfort Zone

A while back a screenwriter friend of mine from the greater California area was whining about how an agency had just turned him down and would not be representing him and his projects.

CUT TO: (sorry…)

A few weeks ago, though, I received another phone call from my friend. He was doing a broken record thing with me about his writing, his projects, not getting people to respond to his read requests, etc. Okay, he was fucking whining again about the lack of movement in his career.

He was looking for advice, so 'advise' I did. I said, "Become your own Producer!!" Actually I do this (with and without the screaming) to nearly every writer who ever asks for advice. Even if they're asking for BBQ tips or recommendations on painting their homes, I'll hit them with the 'become your own Producer' line. I can't turn it off sometimes. But this time my friend was frustrated enough to take that advice to heart – in a BIG way.

One week after our phone call he had a Director attached to

Wallflowers Need Not Apply

his current project (A Director with credits and a USC Film School grad). The Director is someone my friend had met at a screenwriting seminar. How did he achieve this seeming lofty task? It's not rocket science. He called his Director acquaintance and asked if he'd like to read the screenplay for the purpose of directing. They had known each other for a while, and the Director was already familiar with the story idea.

About 6 months prior to this all transpiring, my friend (no names, sorry, don't want to jinx him) had pitched this screenplay idea to a Producer in Hollywood. This was a Producer with deals set up at 2 studios. That Producer liked the concept idea, asked for a copy of the screenplay…and was not heard from again – even after a few follow up calls from my bud.

But that was 6 months ago, long before my friend grew a spine.

The day after he got the Director interested, my friend called this same Producer back and advised him that he had a Director attached and they were moving forward, trying to get this project off the ground. Four hours later, that same Producer called my friend back to say, "I love your script. How can I get involved?"

Sounds crazy, right? This is how things can begin to happen for you when you become your own Producer. This situation points directly to the old Hollywood adage: "You don't make a movie, a movie happens."

My friend was on a roll.

With the assist from the Director, who is well connected (yeah, more networking!), 3 other Producers are now interested in perusing the screenplay and the project as a whole. This is not an uncommon practice, having several Producers/and/or Production Companies partner to get the film made. And you know what? My friend went 3 for 3 with the other Producers – 3 calls, 3 'yes, I'd like to look into this' replies.

The bottom line is that my friend has a Director attached, and 4 Producers interested in his project -- Crazy, but true.

As my friend puts it, "I now understand that taking drastic measures is an act of a person who truly believes in their material."

Drastic? I don't think so. I think this is exactly what you need to be doing if you are that passionate about your work. And does all of this effort by my friend guarantee a completed film? Nope. There's money to be raised, stars to entice, etc. But the movie making process has to begin somewhere. Only you can make a career in this business happen for yourself.

Oh, and I am VERY proud of my friend, too.

Chapter 19

The Authentic Writer

Ah, to censor, or not to censor? Here's my answer.

Fuck that!

Self-imposed censorship should be a non-issue when you write specs. You must strive for as much "authenticity" as you can conjure. Authentic material allows for the possibility that the reader will buy completely into your story, because they'll be more aware of the world you're bringing them into. They're likely already familiar with the setting.

Have your characters smoke – if it's in their character profile to do so. Have them swear their fucking asses off – if it's in their character to do that. Of course, the flip side is to have a character that wants very badly to smoke, swear, whatever, but holds them back – until they finally explode. That can be an entertaining way to write the character, as well.

Some writers are afraid to place brand name products/businesses into their screenplays. Don't be shy, if you want a location to be a Starbuck's call it Starbuck's – or if it's really bothering you, call the location a Starbuck's-like Coffee Shop. That's a little namby-pamby for me but if it works for you, use it. If a character drives a Chevy, call it a Chevy. An Assistant Director may hate you when they have to break down the script and locate an actual Starbuck's to film in, but I'd bet the farm that after the screenplay is green-lit most of these details would be hammered out (through the production lawyers).

I once met a writer who was appalled by something I had written in one of my screenplays. The Antagonist was a really bad dude, and to show this I had him do some very bad things (and he smoked, too). The writer said to me after reading the screenplay, "But what will people think of you?"

Think of me? I'm not the bad dude - the bad dude's on paper. I don't CARE what a reader thinks of me. I want to know what they think of the screenplay. If you're that reticent about allowing yourself (and your characters) to swing for the fences, maybe it's time to reexamine your writing career. Let all that PC bullshit go and see where your story leads you. You could wind up with a much funnier, or darker, piece – and your material will definitely be more "real."

Now back to authenticity as it relates to brand names. I say put them in your screenplay. If a studio is going to make your film, the lawyers, and marketing people are going to go over the thing with a fine-tooth comb, looking for potential problems/and/or/marketing angles (product placement) that may arise. Your Starbuck's may become a Pete's Coffee shop, etc., etc.

If you make a deal on that spec, the chances are (very!) good that the screenplay will be rewritten (several times). If you're

Wallflowers Need Not Apply

asked to cut some of the smoking, swearing, and brand names, to appease the Producer – do it – that's your job. But at that point, you'll be getting paychecks to do your job.

Write "authentic" stuff.

And, yes, you can pander to the PC Police just as much as you can pander to the 'dark side.' Just be true to yourself and be true to your characters.

Chapter 20

Writers Fright

Like writer's block, writer's fright is as equally debilitating.

Writers fright?

Yeah, the condition whereby you work and work to complete drafts of spec screenplays but are afraid to show them to anyone with any real knowledge of screenwriting. Sure it's great to get positive feedback from Mom, and Cousin Sue, but are they really giving you objective, and solid notes? It's highly doubtful.

Writers fright also manifests itself in people who have completed screenplays but are afraid to contact Production Companies with the hopes of actually selling their work. Hey, if you're a hobbyist, that's cool. But if you're attempting to become a professional screenwriter, what in the fuck are you waiting for?

Other forms of writers fright are evident in individuals who tell the world that they are screenwriters but have never written a screenplay, or at least one they can actually show you. When asked if you can read their work, there are the folks who will always reply, "Well, I'm going through a polish right now." Sure

Wallflowers Need Not Apply

you are...

I guess that I can't really blame the 'fright writers' for being afraid. This is an incredibly difficult business to get into and stay afloat in. So, should new screenwriters be fearful of the screenwriting unknowns? Yes.

Should it stop true writers from trying to get into the business?

Never!

You don't know if you have the goods unless you give it a true shot. I recently watched an interview with a working screenwriter who stated something to the effect of, 'Being good at screenwriting is like being able to throw a 90 mile per hour fast ball. Not everyone can do it, and the ones who can have to work on their game/craft to get more control.'

You'll never know if you can throw 90mph unless you try. And if you do choose to move forward in the screenwriting world, you have to have the guts to go full out toward your career goals.

The best way to work your way through writers fright is to have solid ammo in your corner. That ammo must be in the form of well written and well thought out spec screenplays. It should be work that screams for attention. Writing that's very visual, that readers can 'see' in their 'mind's eye' as they zip through your pages. You need to write screenplays that millions and millions of paying customers can't wait to see. (Of course, I'm speaking here to the writers who are trying to make it in the Hollywood-world of screenwriting/filmmaking).

This brings me to the ugly flip side of writer's fright. It's something that's a bit more insidious, really. And that's 'writer's overconfidence.' Oh, yeah, we've all seen it. Hell, I've probably been guilty of it myself.

You believe that you've written some of the greatest stuff ever. No one can even come close to your spec. It'll be purchased in a nanosecond the moment it hits the market.

Yeah, well, it's a good thing to be self-assured, but as with any 'talent' related competition (and screenwriting and selling screenplays IS as competitive as it gets), usually the ones that are the most flamboyant and cock-sure are the ones who tank. Have you ever watched the early rounds of American Idol? To me, that's the real show. Watching the crazy knuckleheads who think they're the next coming of (insert name of favorite singer here) strut their inane stuff believing that they're at the top of their game. It's extremely entertaining to watch in that train-wreck-sort-of-way isn't it?

So, the best ways to overcome writers fright and the writers overconfidence maladies are to own solid specs that have been objectively ripped apart and put back together, and to remain confident, but not lunatic fringe confident. And it never hurts to also acquire a few excellent LA or NYC industry connections.

Chapter 21

You Know What?

You've all heard it, "Write what you know."

But what does that mean?

I actually enjoy meeting new writers, so please don't misunderstand what I'm about to type. I volunteer my time to the conferences and film festivals, so there's no pay involved. I'm never there to hawk books or my nonexistent script analysis services (maybe now, though. I kid!).

I remember at one such conference I had a young man approach me and want to talk about 'writing what you know.' So he said, "I'm a delivery driver for (we'll call it) FEDUPS, and I wrote a screenplay. I'd like to pitch it to you."

Me, "Cool, what's it about?"

"It's about a FEDUPS driver and what it's really like at my work. You know all the stuff that happens during the work day."

Me, "Is it a comedy?"

Him, "Nope."

Me – gulp!

You guessed it. Apparently he literally wrote what he knew. Always remember, just because it happened to you, doesn't necessarily make it interesting to others.

I remember taking a special interest in this FEDUPS guy. I could see that he was losing his confidence as he pitched his idea. I must have been making pained faces, too. Hey, FEDUPS dude, if you're reading this, sorry about the faces. They were totally involuntary.

So I tried to boost his spirits and spark his imagination a bit. I said something to the effect of, "What if your FEDUPS driver/protagonist has a route in a horrible neighborhood, and the violence and shit he sees on a daily basis begins getting to him. He decides to do something about it. He begins calling the cops every time he sees trouble. But when the cops can't seem to help, his emotions boil over and he becomes a proactive vigilante for the good of the neighborhood people. He starts kicking ass and cleaning up the neighborhood on his own."

Twisted? Maybe, who knows? (Too bad Chuck Bronson isn't still available)

Boring? I don't think so. There could be a lot at stake for the FEDUPS driver and the good neighbors.

The above example, to me, is a form of 'writing what you know' and using your imagination to take your story to a more conflicted and exciting level.

<u>Wallflowers Need Not Apply</u>

But for me, 'writing what you know' is more about utilizing all your life experiences, good/bad; emotional/boring – whatever – to create a screenplay people would pay to see.

I don't know anything about computer science, in fact, I'm kind of a technophobe, but I could write an emotional story about a tech-head who is in crises as it relates to his family. We've almost all experienced family strife in our lives. I can research the tech stuff – but the human side of it – I know. So that's more 'writing what you know.'

Chapter 22

This Is Not Novel Work

I've had the chance to read several new writers' work over the past years, and I'm always amazed by how much novelistic bullshit I see. I don't want to single any one person out, because, well, there were hundreds of writers who made this error.

Novelistic, how?

Basically a descriptive action line should not hold an internal character thought or an extensive character history. In most cases, if we can't see it on camera, you shouldn't be typing it on the page. Here's a brief (bad) description example: "BETTY CROCKER, who will be 22 years old on May 14, cute and precocious, pulls a freshly baked cake from the oven. The baking skills Betty learned in the 7th grade while attending Franklin Junior High in Madison, Wisconsin, has served her well in her avocation. Betty's Mom used to always tell her…(etc., etc.)"

Holy shit! Not good.

How do we know Betty's past? How in the world is a director, cast, and crew going to film *'the baking skills Betty learned in*

Wallflowers Need Not Apply

7th grade while attending Franklin Junior High in Madison, Wisconsin, has served her well in her avocation"?? A screenplay is the blue print and framework for a film. It is not a novel. If material is not seen or heard during the film, it shouldn't be on the page. If the information is that imperative to your story, you must figure out a way to either work it into the descriptions to be filmed, or into the dialogue – or get rid of it altogether.

Okay, so maybe once in a great while you can place a brief 'novelistic' tidbit into your work – a word or three - but what I've been seeing is that the Newbies are doing it over and over, throughout the entire screenplay. And this all got me thinking. Have these writers even read a screenplay? Have they taken any weekend screenwriting courses or attended seminars? Have they read a few screenwriting how-to books that explain the basics of the craft? Please don't misunderstand me -- I'm not condemning the people themselves. These are some very cool folks, who are intelligent, and worldly – yet they say they're screenwriters, but exhibit very little of those screenwriting traits on paper. They're not arrogant people. They're not thumbing their noses at course work and saying, 'I know what I'm doing, and I don't need to learn anymore.' At least I don't think so…

We, as writers, must dig deep and work to the best of our abilities to ensure that all the components of our screenplays are effective. Being novelistic is not helping your cause. In fact, the professional readers I know will 'circular file' that novelistic screenplay after reading a page or two. No shit. It's tough enough out here to make a deal with an excellent screenplay in hand, so why blow your chances by not following the simple tenets of the craft?

I'm just not sure where all the novelistic stuff is coming from –
But please make it go away.

Chapter 23

Excuses, Excuses…?

Some of the more seasoned screenwriters out there may look on this chapter as me trying to paint a pretty face on what can be an ugly reality. They may consider this my version of making excuses for those of you who have received a "pass" from a Production Company – especially in the latter part of the calendar year (I'll explain this later).

And I can deal with that…

If you don't know, a "pass" means the Production Company is not interested in your work, and they are passing. Yes, the vast majority of screenplays that get a "pass" are given the boot because they're total shit (admittedly a few of my own specs are included in this category, as well).

But some of the Newbies in screenwriting land may not take into account that there are only a finite amount of funds available at each Production Company in each and every fiscal year. Of course, if the Prodco has had a couple of good years, they'll be able to buy up more property to develop. So, generally speaking, most Prodco's money trees don't eternally generate new leafs.

From the biggest company in town to the one with a couple of hundred grand in their coffers, they're businesses, and they have to be run as such, or they will fail.

So, yes, it is possible that a Production Company actually likes your screenplay, but is unable to option it because they don't have the funding. It happens. Sure, they can try and string you along until they get more resources in the bank to cover the option/purchase. And if they truly love your screenplay, they'll try just about anything to keep you in their fold.

And see, if the Prodco is stringing you along, trying to see if they can pick up your property when they're more financially sound, could it be that they are the ones making the excuses?

Wallflowers Need Not Apply

Chapter 24

On The Nose

Do you want your screenplays to read more like the pros from the get-go? Here's a simple tip to try on your next draft.

Don't write dialogue that describes what we are seeing in your descriptions. If you have one character offering a beer to another, you don't want to state the obvious with a, "Want a beer?" line of dialogue. We, as the reading/viewing audience, know it's a beer. We have seen beer before (some more than others). Just describe the one character either handing the beer to the other, or saying (if you have to), "Want one?"

"Show," through descriptions more, and say less through dialogue MUCH, much less. Much. If we see it, don't say it.

Most new screenwriters could go through their drafts and cut gobs and gobs of dialogue. Most of it, you'll find, is not even necessary.

You think I'm off base?

Try rewriting a scene from your current draft by showing more, and saying less through dialogue. You'll immediately see what I'm talking about. What you'll discover is that you'll be writing a movie. Moving pictures.

They're not called talkies anymore.

You really don't want to mark your screenplay as amateurish from page one, so stop with the on the nose dialogue. And the "trick" to get past writing on the nose is to stop writing so fricking much dialogue in the first place. Instead, describe more using an economy of descriptive words.

And the beautiful part of writing less on the nose dialogue and more description is that it'll open your screenplays up to adding much more subtext through the characters actions. Subtext is good, folks. It can (hopefully) complicate the visual nature of your screenplay. So you'll soon end up with a screenplay that's not so dialogue driven, and one that is layered with sub-textural (is that even a word?) action.

<u>Wallflowers Need Not Apply</u>

Chapter 25

Flame Free Bridges

Are you a wimp if you choose to not stand up for yourself and burn a potential Hollywood bridge after presumably being 'dissed' by some LA or NYC hotshot Producer/Executive?

You've contacted a Producer/Executive in LA or NYC and he/she has read your work, liked it, but has kind-a-sort-a strung you along, not really ever making a yeah or nay decision on your screenplay. They're always putting you off and saying, "Let me get back to you." And this noncommittal activity has gone on for, let's say, almost a year.

Been there – and I wanted to rip their lungs out for teasing me for so long. I would love to tell some evasive schmuck to piss up the proverbial rope -- but I won't, and here's why.

One of the mottos I've lived by is this: "No is an acceptable answer." The reason I arrived at this mantra was from years of trying to speak with investors who were "interested" in funding Indie films. Lots of money people are interested but have one hell of a time parting with their coinage. Understandable, I guess.

The evil twin to the "No" is the "Maybe."

"Maybes" (as explained at the start of this chapter) suck. A maybe is a total time waster. Especially when trying to raise money from potential movie investors. You don't want to stop the process of getting your stuff out into the world. A "No" means you can instantly move on to your next investor, Producer, etc., without pause.

But, with every rule…

An Austin based screenwriter bud of mine, a very comical man, and an excellent writer in my estimation, recently had a "Maybe" come back to give him a big fat smooch full on the lips.

My Austin friend had made an excellent contact with a very highly regarded old guard Hollywood family, a connection he made through perseverance and simply having the guts to call on the company in question and pitch the hell out of his story. He never wavered, never backed down. He got his read – and waited, and waited. He actually forgot all about the contact, which was probably for the best, because—

Recently radio silence turned into all out activity for this Austinite (Austonian?). The Producer/Executive in question just came out of several months of hibernation, apologized for not getting back sooner, and wants to move forward with the screenplay project.

Lesson? Patience is good sometimes…

Sometimes…

Wallflowers Need Not Apply

Put that lighter fluid away, ace.

Chapter 26

Enter The Variables

"I've written a solid dramatic screenplay. It's my sixth effort. I've received positive feedback from a professional script consultant and writer friends, but I keep getting passed over by Production Companies. Help!"

First off -- congratulations on getting the reads!

Help?

Not sure how much help I can be. But I may be able to explain some of your anxiety away. Hopefully it'll help you sleep better at night, and focus, so you can keep writing, creating, and submitting/marketing your stuff.

Analogy time (apologies in advance…).

Screenwriting is like very few other professions. It's not akin to, say, accounting. In accounting you could go to college, study every now and then, wind up with a "D" GPA and still be able to find a gig, maybe, somewhere - Probably as my accountant.

In screenwriting, you could be a top-notch writer, crafting

excellent page after page, and yet, never make a dime from your efforts. Ever.

Subjectivity, of course, comes into play when creating "art." Especially when it may take $50 million or so to see that your screenplay comes to fruition. That's some heavily influenced "$ubjectivity."

And here's another thing to consider…

Production Companies are normally (usually!!) extremely focused on looking at certain types of screenplays. The company most likely will have a set of parameters they work within to find what they want to produce. Your screenplay idea may simply not fall into those parameters. From your log line, they may have thought it did, but once read, the Production Company knew the fit wasn't right.

That may not be a reflection on your writing (maybe) -- it's just the way it is.

Dipping back into analogies…

Let's say creating screenplays was likened to building houses. Your writing of that spec screenplay is similar to the building of a speculative new home. And as a builder you craft the most beautiful "McMansion," complete with a 20 foot high entry way, sweeping staircases, marble floors, granite counter tops in the kitchen, et al.

And you build the house in the middle of a trailer park (nothing against trailer parks – "visual" for effect only).

You see where I'm going here – the same scenario could be

switched – plopping a brand spanking new trailer home in the middle of a tree lined, high-end, gated subdivision.

Some things simply don't fit well with the other.

I'm not saying you wrote a "trailer home," but don't let the Production Companies 'pass' take you down into those writers-angst-ridden dumps.

Stay with it – create, keep writing new specs as you market this current one, and hope that either your "trailer home" or your "McMansion" winds up in the right neighborhood.

Chapter 27

Take It Or Leave It

I've read a lot of screenplays by Professionals, and Newbie writers alike. They've all been looking for my honest opinion about their work. I'm quite honored to think that my opinion even counts…

So—

If I know the person fairly well, and time allowing, I don't mind taking a look at all. It's the being honest part on the back end of that reading process that can get dicey sometimes. And it's usually the Newbies I have trouble with.

I can't really blame them for being defensive; the Newbies, that is. And they can get very fucking defensive. The screenplay I'm perusing may be the first or second screenplay they've ever written. It's their baby, and their pride and joy. And I may be about to tell them that their little darling doesn't photograph so great.

Without being rude, I simply tell them the things that work (for me), and the things that don't work. It's my opinion, so take it with a big fat grain of salt, my friends.

Simply take the notes, but please don't argue with the reader and tell them how they don't understand your vision. If the reader didn't get it, you probably didn't write the work well enough for them to understand it in the first place.

The Newbie asked for a read, the reader gave them what they requested – an honest opinion. Please don't argue with the person you asked an opinion of. Take the notes, and move on. Believe me; you're not going to be able to "argue" your way to a more positive reaction from the reader. Your defensive nature will simply shut them down, and their honest feedback will evaporate. The notes aren't a personal attack.

Hopefully the reader's notes will help refocus and hone your rewriting process. And we all know that the rewriting is the real writing. That's why you had someone else read the screenplay to begin with, to get honest notes, right? Simply listen, and take it all in. If you have a few people read your screenplay and they're all saying the same negative things, it may be time to rework your stuff. Something is obviously off in those parts of your screenplay.

When I have people read my stuff, I specifically ask them what they thought of the spots I KNOW I'm having trouble with. I want to stir up that bee's nest of notes. Being able to be objective with your own work is crucial to a writer's growth. It allows you to recognize problem areas even before you send your stuff out into the world. And even then it's not going to solve all the problems that all those various readers' eyes may see.

If only one or two people harp on one or two varying points in

Wallflowers Need Not Apply

the work, try to keep those notes in the back of your head as you rewrite -- but you're probably closer to being on the right track.

If you're afraid of what others are going to say about your screenwriting ability, simply don't show your work to anyone. But we all know you'll never get anywhere with that kind of defeatist attitude.

Allow your screenwriter's skin to thicken, get your reads, take the notes (without rebuttal!), and begin the rewriting. You can save up all of that writer's angst to argue with a Producer after the work is sold and you're getting paid.

Chapter 28

What A Character

As I create the characters in my work, and I go through the extensive note taking process that will eventually become my screenplay, I try and give the characters distinct speaking styles.

One person may speak more proper English than the next, or one may have the nasty habit of stopping-

Man, it is fucking hot today.

-in mid sentence and starting a new train of thought.

What I like to do is simply listen to other people speak in public, pick up on speech patterns, mimic them and try to capture those various speech patterns on the page.

Why have a character say "It's okay," when they can say "S'okay." "S'okay" shows, to me, that maybe, just maybe, we're not dealing with the most cultured son of a bitch.

Hone in on people you know - Mash-up various speech patterns that you hear daily to create interesting characters. (Lawyer made me type this disclaimer: Just don't write about the specific

Wallflowers Need Not Apply

lives of people you know whose speech patterns you're ripping on – unless you have proper releases – or you're really, really good at disguising them.)

When I was a kid my Dad owned a bar. And on Sunday mornings, when I was 13 or 14 years old, I would go with him to clean up after a raucous Saturday night and prep the place for the busy week ahead. The city had a "Blue law" whereby the bars couldn't open until Noon on Sundays, so the work had to be done fairly quickly.

This was a shot and a beer kind of place (no fern could survive there). As High Noon approached, and as I completed my chores of replacing empty kegs, mopping floors, and stocking beer bottles in the bar coolers, the "Regulars" would stand outside looking through that little diamond shaped window in the front door. They'd be making faces, displaying their wrist watches and tapping on them to show us that it was already noon (somewhere). Their efforts never provoked my Dad into opening early, though. He liked to keep his business license intact.

When twelve o'clock struck, my Dad would open the place up and the 4 or 5 regulars would step in and sidle up to the bar, order their shots of Rye, bottles of Old Style, and whatnot. And I would have a field day taking in their conversations!

The speech patterns, obviously alcoholically altered, were incredible to listen to. The pacing, the invectives they would affectionately spew at each other. It was beautiful. And great stuff for any aspiring writer to – pardon - drink in.

So, yeah, there are ways to make your characters all sound different. Go to Starbuck's without your buds – and just listen to other people converse. Sit on a bench at a busy mall and take in the arguing couple as they walk past, or the mother keeping her kids in line, the teens trying to be cool, etc., etc.

And just as you would stay true to your characters story line (character arc, etc.) - don't stray too far from the speech patterns you've crafted for them.

Chapter 29

"Original" Thought

Rant to follow: I see the same shit from new writers time and time again.

I'd argue that all of the screenplays we're creating (spec-ing) are obviously derived from some prior occurrence, experience, or story we've been exposed to. Nothing is truly "original."

But that being typed, why do I see so many new writers "adapting" old stories that are currently in the public domain? I know "Hollywood" recycles shit like crazy, but why would you? You know who I'm talking to, Miss., "Hey, I'm going to re-work Beowulf!" Or Mr., "I want to write my version of Cinderella!"

Fucking stop!

If I see another Vlad the Impaler rehash, I'm gonna puke. And I've seen plenty, unfortunately.

Leave it be, and try to craft specs that have a hint of originality, would ya! To me, rehashing old stories for your specs shows outright laziness.

Now, if you work your ass off and create an original spec (as original as you can), and that gets you a paid assignment to write some recycled bullshit story for a Hollywood Producer, wonderful! That's the way things work sometimes. But please, simply try to show some sort of originality from the start of your career.

Chapter 30

Got Guts?

If you're gambling away your free time by venturing into the screenwriting world, I'd say yes, to some degree, you have the fortitude needed to work in this industry.

But simply dipping your toes into the screenwriting game, most often, won't guarantee any bit of success as a screenwriter. Hell, there's no guarantee at all that you'll ever make it in this business – ever! However, there are simple steps that may propel you forward. This is so outrageously simple yet, generally typing, the majority of the new writers out there will pull up short before they even give themselves a true shot at this thing of ours.

You have to get your writing work out into the world. You have to be attempting to make personal contacts with Producers in Hollywood or NYC to see if they're interested in reading your screenplays.

"Of course we want that!"

Yeah, sure…

You'd be amazed at how many new writers simply don't market their wares. I've had the pleasure of being on panels at several film festivals, and I'm always running into frightened screenwriters at these events. They'll tell me of how afraid they are of letting their little babies fly from the nest and be torn to pieces by Hollywood. In fact, I'd venture a guess that about 70% of the new writers I speak with are fearful of marketing themselves and their writing. Sounds crazy, right? You know what, come to think of it; it's probably closer to 75%.

And I'm not talking about posting your screenplays on pay sites where top tier Producers are allegedly stopping by to read and be amazed by your expertise. I'm talking about making personal contacts among Hollywood or NYC Production Companies – and high profile Production Companies, too. Subscribe to a service like the Hollywood Creative Directory, or ImdbPro.com, where you'll be able to research Production Companies, find the companies who have made films similar to yours in the past, and contact them with simple email queries.

Recently, a fearless new email buddy of mine did just this. Check that. He wasn't completely fearless. He was dragging his feet a might at first, but he rallied in a big way. He has a very off-beat and quirky screenplay that he knows could be a tough sell in Hollywood, but he believes in his writing so much that he went WAY out on a limb and approached a highly (HIGHLY) successful Director/Producer (info he found through ImdbPro. com. And no, I'm not a paid endorser).

My friend wrote a very simple, yet compelling query email. Basically one sentence about himself, the genre, the log line, the title, and he signed off with his contact info. I mean a very short and sweet email. You must realize that a lot of the Producers you'll be approaching (and this applies for agents and managers, too) work from handheld mobile devices, so they'll appreciate short, sweet, and kick ass queries.

Guess what?

The Director/Producer contacted my buddy himself. And he wants to read his screenplay.

Is a sale guaranteed? Well, of course not.

But man-o-man did my new bud step out of his comfort zone to get his work read. Scary? You bet. Necessary? Fuck yeah!!

Chapter 31

Why Do You Do It?

Write screenplays, that is…

Is it for the money? Is it for the fame? (Must suppress giggle) Or do you write to maybe attract the opposite (or same) sex?

Or do you simply have a passion to create?

I'm sure if some shrink dug deep within the recesses of my peabrain, they could figure out why I stared writing. In fact, about a year ago, I met a very prominent Psychiatrist at a party. When he learned that I was a screenwriter, and had never been to a Psychiatrist in my life, he offered me a free session.

My response?

Verbatim (really!), "Are you fucking crazy? I need all this shit in my head to compete in the screenwriting game. I don't want to lose that edge."

His response was a hearty laugh. He actually agreed that I should keep doing what I'm doing (floundering through life, I presume).

Wallflowers Need Not Apply

I do know this. I've been writing my entire life. I've always been creating little stories (sorry, Mom & Dad). It's just something that's ingrained in my genetic code. Why fight it?

Why do you write?

Chapter 32

Hello, It's Me

I just finished the first portion of my latest assignment and I'm coming up for air.

In several recent conversations, other writers have asked me how, when I'm out and about (or driving), and not in reach of pen and paper, do I remember the story ideas that continuously pop into my head.

Simple.

I've programmed my cell phone to – well – call my cell phone. I list the "contact" as "Record." So it doesn't matter where I am (except for airplanes, of course). I can always leave a verbal note and retrieve it later when I have pen and paper or laptop at my disposal. Most cell phones also have a record function. But to me calling myself is much more romantic.

No cell phone?

Always try to have quarters in your pocket and find a payphone (if that's even possible in your neck of the woods) so you can call

Wallflowers Need Not Apply

home and leave yourself the note on your answering machine/ voice mail.

No home phone?

You should really consider moving out of Amish country if you're going to give yourself a chance at making it in the screenwriting game...

Chapter 33

Genre Specific

"Is it better to hone a specific screenwriting genre, or is there an advantage to 'shot gunning' your spec scripts into various genres (comedy, drama, horror, etc.)?"

There's probably no right or wrong answer to this question other than you should create what excites you as a screenwriter.

Is this a copout answer?

Not really…

If you're simply trying to write a comedy, for instance, because you see that comedy is selling like crazy at present, but you don't have a funny bone in your body? Yeah, that can be a problem. You're probably setting yourself up for a painful, and time consuming, failure. You could always chalk up the time wasted on finding out that you're not that funny as a learning experience, right?

I write mostly comedy (dark and otherwise), but even my comedy has twinges of drama. From drama comes comedy. Conversely, the dramas I write tend to have some comedy in them. But sure, you could "shot gun" write into various genres, why not?

You may discover that you're really more of a drama writer than a comedy writer, or horror writer instead of a rom-com writer. I'd add that you might want to try and stay true to yourself and your tastes, sensibilities, and passions, though. I bet you'll discover that you stay within a genre or two when you do this. Life's too short to be writing something that you dislike just because you think it'll sell, unless you can pull down $750,000 from your "wasted efforts." Then all bets are off.

See - no right or wrong answer…

Chapter 34

Trend + Luck = Opportunity

"Should I write to trends in the spec sales market?"

A great question…

The short answer, for me, is always going to be no.

By the time you recognize that "what's selling" trend, and you complete a screenplay in that genre, said trend could be tossed aside like yesterdays – well - screenplays. Certainly you can try to ride a trend wave and hack your way into a screenplay that may or may not sell. I'd wish you all the best with that (snark intended).

For me, the solid approach would be to keep after your writing by creating spec after excellent spec. Create marketable ideas that speak to your passions as a writer and a human being. What you may discover is that that you've positioned yourself to be in the forefront of a trend. You'll also, most likely, become a much better writer in the process.

Create your own luck by continuously producing an excellent

Wallflowers Need Not Apply

product. Keep writing – keep your eye on marketing – be passionate about your product - and keep after it. What you're working on now may not be in vogue today, but it may sell down the road sometime. You could, someday, find yourself riding the crest of the next trend's wave.

That is so gnarly, dude.

Chapter 35

Show Me Yours

If you're reading this book, the chances are good (I'm hoping) that you've completed a screenplay or two (or three).

Excellent!

Now, what are you doing to get your work in front of people who are actually able to make decisions on optioning/purchasing your screenplays? Are you emailing/calling Production Companies? Making regular excursions to LA or NYC to meet with anyone you possibly can? Are you going to pitch fests? Are you attending writers conferences, workshops, and/or seminars?

Basically - are you networking your ass off?

Your chances of success can be diminished if you're not getting yourself out there. I know it's scary, but meeting and having people read your work is necessary if you want to have a legitimate shot at this business.

I hear this, or variations of the following, all the time from writers who are a bit gun shy. This is one of their excuses for not sending their work out to be read.

"I went to a pitch fest recently and was flabbergasted by the age of the young man hearing my pitch. He was no more than 23 years old! What does he know about anything?"

Welcome to Hollywood, my friend…

That 20-something executive you may encounter, if not one of the bosses, is at least a gatekeeper at the Production Company. Who do you think you're writing your spec scripts for? These are the fine folks who will be taking a first look at your screenplay and either tossing it, or pushing it up the ladder. This pretty much applies at most talent agencies, as well. Get over it, and get used to it.

Chapter 36

Zip It!

You've done it. You've put yourself out there and made some connections in the biz. You've worked your ass off, networked, and set up a meeting with an Executive or Producer who has read something of yours, and now they're interested in you as a writer. Things are good.

Now it's the day of the meeting, and you're a nervous wreck. But it's good to be alive and writing.

So you're in the meeting, and things are going swimmingly. The Producer/Executive talks about how they appreciated the work they've already read, but the screenplay that you wrote is just not right for them. They say something like, "What else do you have completed?" Bam, there it is. And you're ready. You hit them with your latest finished screenplay idea. You lay it out there, using a snappy log line to gauge their level of interest. It's a brief, yet, compelling, quick pitch.

The Producer/Executives eyebrows shoot up, and a crooked smile creases their lips. And then they say, "I like it."

Wallflowers Need Not Apply

Awesome!

What do you do now?

Producers/Executives don't have a lot of time, so I'd highly suggest coming back with something very simple like, "Great, I'll go ahead and send you a copy." Now here's the difficult part for most writers, let alone human beings, after having something as exciting as this play out for them.

After the Producer/Executive has agreed to read your new work, you need to do really only one thing.

Shut the fuck up!

Do NOT talk anymore about the screenplay that you'll be sending to them. Drop it. Leave it hanging in the breeze. It's completely okay. If they've already decided on reading your latest screenplay, you can only cause them to back pedal by talking any further about the idea. You never know when something you utter may turn them off. You did your first sales job - you got them to say 'yes' to a read.

"But what do I talk about, instead?"

Talk about anything BUT the screenplay that they've just agreed to read. I was once in a Producers office and the above scenario played out after only a few minutes, and what did I do? I noticed all these cool models and mini-statues of characters from their past films assembled around the office. So I struck up a conversation about those little knick-knacks – and NOT about what they had already agreed to read.

Talk about the weather, sports, whatever, but do not talk about what they've already agreed to read.

Allow the screenplay to speak for itself when it arrives at their offices in the agreed upon manner (email or snail mail). Don't overplay your verbal hand in the office, you'll only allow yourself to say something that may turn the Producer/Executive off. You overplay your hand, you may be looking at a, "You know, on second thought," coming back at you.

"What if they don't agree to read it right away and ask for more of a pitch?"

That's when you launch into a more detailed pitch – again – with the focus on getting them to actually agree to read the screenplay. If at any point during this longer pitch they agree to read your work, STOP the pitch, and move the conversation into another direction. I had a meeting once where I started the secondary pitch by saying, "Okay, you've read that last screenplay. You know how I write. The next one I'll send you is about a father/son bank robbery team." The Producer smiled and nodded. Bam – done. Shut the fuck up!

"But what if something I don't mention in my pitch turns them off when they finally do read my work?"

The Producer/Executive's time investment may be on your side at that point. Hell, it's all a crapshoot, you know. But if you are able to get your screenplay into their hands, and they like the overall story line, and the way you executed it, some minor detail may not be enough to nix the deal.

I know this may all sound rather silly, but I've seen firsthand how writers can mess things up by over pitching an idea. Your

Wallflowers Need Not Apply

initial idea got the Producer/Executives attention, and garnered a "Yeah, let me read that" response. Ride that 'yes' to a read, and zip the lip, my friend.

Chapter 37

ABC's

I like to set time aside for "log lining" sessions. It's how I conjure up story ideas.

You know what a log line is, right? It's the one or two sentence description of your screenplay.

With pad and pen in hand, I crank up some tunes, let my mind drift, and come up with story ideas. First blush log lines. Some I keep, most I toss. Of those I keep, I usually have not only the log line, but also some corresponding notes for each. So I have a fairly decent grasp of those stories. This, of course, is in addition to the screenplays that I've completed.

I've discovered that it's very important to have ideas on hand when you meet with Producers. Can't speak for you, but the Producers I meet always ask, "What else are you working on?" Now I realize that what I'm about to write sort of goes against the popular thought process on this topic. Our paranoid brains may think, "No don't let Producers know about our precious story lines. They'll steal them."

Wallflowers Need Not Apply

Well, they may, but chances are they won't.

If you're in a meeting with a Producer the odds are they've read something of yours and they either like the screenplay itself (awesome!), and/or they appreciate you as a writer. Allow me a Simon Cowell moment here – most spec screenplays don't sell. My apologies if I crushed that dream for you. However, because of that spec you've worked so diligently on, the Producer may want to work with you on an idea of theirs, or possibly see if you have any other ideas that may be of interest to them. See where I'm going with this?

You want to be ready. You want to 'Always Be Creating' (big shout out to Mr. Mamet and Glenngarry Glen Ross).

The "Hollywood" Producer is searching for - ever seeking – pleading for – demanding (!) marketable ideas. They seek high concept gems that they can pitch to a studio or investor in a sentence or two. And that pitch will hopefully garner a positive reaction (I believe the official vernacular in these instances is - Cha-Ching!).

Okay, so the Producer passed on your spec, but now they go ahead and ask the inevitable "what else do you have" question. That's a GREAT thing for them to ask. That most likely means they trust you as a writer (yes!) and now they're seeing if you can wow them with another marketable idea. The more marketable ideas that you can create raise your chances of having a shot at this screenwriting game. Simple, right?

I have a Producer acquaintance that is always looking for writers to work with. Hell, I don't know of many Producers who aren't looking for writers to work with. So, I recommended a new writer

I knew to this Producer. The new guy in question is the real deal in my estimation otherwise I wouldn't be recommending him.

They met and the new guy was asked the "What else do you have" question. Like a good Boy Scout the new guy was prepared, and gave the Producer his impassioned most excellent try with a couple of his bestest ideas ever – and was quickly shot down in flames…

Why?

In the Producers opinion, the new guy's future ideas didn't fit into his definition of marketable.

The Producers I know all have a finely tuned laser focus on the stuff they want to be working on. Your idea may not, in most cases, actually, fit into their focused efforts. Yes, this is a subjective industry that we're all clamoring to be part of, but you must skew your story line thought process to "marketable" if you want to give yourself a chance at making it in the "Hollywood" screenwriting game. Turn your story lines on their heads, toss them, and spin them, until you come up with marketable hooks that a Producer can sell up the ladder to a larger Producer or Studio.

My new writer friend is one hell of a scribe, so he's not totally out this Producer's line of sight, and he's learned a very valuable lesson. But the new guy is now posed with the question of the screenwriting ages…

"Do I continue on my current path, writing the story lines I've already developed, or do I put the time in to work on more marketable fare?"

Wallflowers Need Not Apply

It's tough out there. But if you're ready for the punches, they tend not to hurt as much.

Chapter 38

Why/What?

Here's the thing. I've written a lot, filmed some, and created a good-sized personal network over the years. This has, thankfully, allowed me to get my work into the right people's hands. I've accumulated a lot of experiences, both good and bad, and I'm simply trying to relay that knowledge to you.

When I started screenwriting, there were no outlets for frank discussions on breaking into the world of screenwriting. No one really spoke about your chances, how difficult it can be, and other tricks of the trade, etc. And you know what? I wish I would've had someone giving me that straight talk then, so I'm giving it to you now hoping that it helps you along your screenwriting way. Screenwriting and the movie business are never really about puppy dogs, sunshine, and rainbows (unless you're constantly getting gigs at Disney).

Chapter 39

Could've Had a V-8

I had an epiphany recently.

You know how all the "experts," or anyone (like me) with a book will say stuff like, "Read great screenplays to see how the pros write, it'll make you a stronger writer?" I know firsthand, because I believe (d) in this advice for a time. And I read a lot of great screenplays.

But now after reading the great ones I say read bad screenplays.

Don't rub your eyes, you read that correctly. Read as many horrible, skin crawlingly bad screenplays as you possibly can. Oh, they're out there. The WGA has 50,000 or so of them pass through their computer files each and every year.

Other than the WGA, there are all sorts of places to find bad screenplays to peruse. I won't mention them by name, but I bet you can find an Internet site or seven where you have to file share and read a number of screenplays so you can get feedback on your work from other new screenwriters. That's seemingly, a good idea, right?

Granted, I'm probably out of line with what I'm about to type but, for shits sake, you do realize that you may be getting "notes" from some 12 year old kid in Schaumburg, Illinois, who just figured out what a protagonist is, right? Take the advice you get from these places for what it's worth.

If we can miraculously become fabulous screenwriters from reading great screenplays, why aren't we all awesome screenwriters?

On the flip side of the 'read great screenplays' adage, when I read a really bad screenplay it makes me want to do a better job with my next project. That bad screenplay makes me strive for more. It forces me to dig a little deeper into story and character. To NOT make the same mistakes that the really bad screenplay has on nearly every page.

Reading bad screenplays forces me to focus on writing the best drafts that I possibly can, and to NOT write on-the-nose dialogue (a biggie, by the way!). It makes me attempt for more visual screenplays, etc. And most times all of this isn't even enough to save my work, but I know I'm heading down the right track. There's one thing most people trying to get into the business never understand. That screenwriters, even after having some success; have to always prove themselves -- Over and over again.

And please, I'm not passing judgment on the people behind the bad screenplays (I may be one of them!). These are some very nice and determined people. They just haven't "gotten it" yet.

See, all those achingly bad screenplays are not created for naught. They die so that other screenplays can live. The bad screenplay

Wallflowers Need Not Apply

is the hero of the screenwriting world.

Chapter 40

Parenthetical Madness

Okay, I was guilty of the following in my early writing days.

Stop with the (parenthetical) use under the character's name in the dialogue portion of your screenplays!

Just stop!

Please, for all that is good in the world of screenwriting, cease and desist with the (parentheticals).

I beg you…

Yeah, yeah, Movie Magic and Final Draft make it reeeeaaal easy to place those little stoppers in the dialogue portion of your pages, but do you realize what damage they're doing to your screenplays?

I don't think so. I call them stoppers for a reason.

(Parentheticals) stop the eye from scanning, folks, it's been confirmed by Optical Engineers at Stanford University (Okay, I just made that up – and see - I stopped you from reading

Wallflowers Need Not Apply

the real article by placing this inside a set of these fucking parentheseseses…).

There is a very simple, yet important, thought process behind eliminating ( ). You do not want to stop the reader from reading. Ever! (Well, until they get to the very end of your screenplay – shit, see, now you have me doing the ( ) thing again!! These ( ) are infectious!)

I only use the ( ) in this chapter to misdirect you, effectively keeping you off balance. Sneaky? Of course, but it's my book. You don't want to misdirect the reader of your screenplay. You want to keep them in the moment and flipping rapidly through the pages. Here's another of my mottos: "Breezy is good."

Try not using any (parentheticals) at all in your next draft. You will immediately see how clean, pristine, and sleek your pages will appear. Sound ridiculous? Ask any Producer or Hollywood reader who's saddled with reading 50 or more screenplays in a week. They'll love you for nixing the dreaded ( ).

"But, but, but…what do I use instead of the (parenthetical)?"

Nothing.

Break up dialogue with brief lines of description. Just use a line of description or a word or two to set the tone of the scene. Maybe add a 'visual' to the scene, something that "shows" what you're trying to communicate. It'll add subtext to the scene. Just use something other than (Angry), (Excited), or (Wryly). Keep it breezy, and do – not – stop – the - eye.

Okay, if you MUST add one or two sets of (parentheticals) into a 100-page screenplay, do it, but no more. No, no, no. Scratch that!

Just stop using (parentheticals) altogether. I'm calling on all screenwriters worldwide to immediately boycott all screenwriting (parentheticals), unless used to denote some sort of technical direction like (VO), or (OS)...But that's it!

I need a (drink)…

Wallflowers Need Not Apply

Chapter 41

Luck Off

I had lunch recently with a screenwriting buddy. He's fairly new to the game and asked me what it's like to have a well-known Production Company read/like/and consider taking on something I've written. I've been fortunate enough to have this type of scenario play out time and time again. He was all bugged-eyed with anticipation as he waited for my reply, probably hoping-upon-hope that I would wax poetically about the feeling of bliss and accomplishment that one can experience—

-- until that "non-deal" falls into oblivion.

It's not a deal until the check clears, so simply having a Production Company show interest, while yes exciting, is pretty much a fairly common occurrence worthy of nothing more than a passing, "Oh, cool." Followed by my daily chores (my beautiful wife is kind a stickler for vacuumed carpets and Swiffered floors…we're seeking counseling).

Unfortunately for me, and I'd guess a good number of other screenwriters who've been at this for a while, most "potential deals" are really non-deals. You're led to believe that someone is hot on your screenplay and then the heat fades as quickly as it flared. I've learned to react in the same fashion to that non-deal falling apart as I do to the possibility of making a deal - With a calm disposition. If I didn't level my head, I'd be punching holes in walls, or worse, writing books about screenwriting.

My buddy then asked me how many times I've had non-deals become nothing-at-all-deals. I had to think about that for a minute. "You mean in the past year?"

Yeah, it's happened to me a bunch of times.

Maybe it's me. Maybe it's my writing. Or maybe it's the fact that the executive revolving doors in Hollywood spin at such a ferocious pace that you can't keep track of all the comings and goings. Perhaps it's a little of all the above?

My screenwriting bud was surprised that non-deals fall away so quickly after the one championing your cause at a Production Company makes his/her exit. He never took into consideration that just because one executive at a company likes your screenplay, that the second they leave the employ of said Production Company, everything they were working on (in most situations) simply goes "poof" into thin air. At least that's how it's panned out for me in those instances. Hopefully for you, you're cranking out the deals left and right. Jealous? Me? Nah…

"But, why wouldn't that executive take your project to his/her new company?"

Well, because a lot of times, when he/she does land at a new company, the new employer is looking for a different type of material, and my stuff may not fit in to their corporate vision.

Wallflowers Need Not Apply

And actually in one case, after I asked my agent if the Producer would be willing to look at my screenplay at his new place of employment, the answer was not one I fully expected -- "Well, his new job is with a Beverly Hills realtor…"

Chapter 42

Blocky Description

There's nothing that stops the Reader's eye quicker than a big, wordy, block of description. And a "stopper" like blocky description can be a read killer.

For a smoother read, try not having blocks of description with more than 4 lines. If you do this your story will flow from the page and not bog the Reader's eye down with a daunting (steaming) lump of heaping text.

More "white space" on the page is the friend of the screenwriter.

And there's another reason for writing description in sections of 4 or fewer lines; it's a way to "direct" the movie in the Reader's imagination. Each 4 or shorter line section of text is actually describing "shots" and "angles" without writing clunky, and way too technical - ANGLE ONs, CLOSE ONs, etc.

As the action of a scene changes point of view in your imagination while you write, you simply make a space and begin a new 4 or fewer line section of description.

Wallflowers Need Not Apply

Example:

INT-DINER-DAY

Formica abounds in the no frills restaurant.

There are four booths and six tables. Jazz music plays from an old radio behind the counter.

The owner, EDDY PETE (35), with a sharp glimmer in his eye, letting you know his lights are on full, places a greasy bowl of beef stew in front of-

RONNY DIKENS

Ronny's fifty years old - and ornery. The loan shark/bookie for the neighborhood sits in the raggedy booth tucking a napkin into his shirt collar.

--End Example.

Here's an important point when first describing a new character, too. Please, please, never bury the new character in the middle of the dreaded "lump of heaping text." There's a chance that the Reader will miss the character all together. It happens, and it can be quite confusing to the Reader.

Begin a new section of description and make sure your new character is introduced as soon as possible (see example above).

Making your screenplay an easier "read" doesn't necessarily equate to simplistic description. Using an economy of words, and the best descriptive words you have access to, will heighten your chances of having your screenplay float to the top of the

Readers "yes" list.

Wallflowers Need Not Apply

Chapter 43

Rub Out The Nub

Okay, so you're cranking out kick ass descriptions and snappy dialogue using an economy of the 'bestest' words you have access to. Your descriptions rarely spill over 4 lines of action (usually staying at 2 lines). Your dialogue is popping, and your pages are looking white, and lean. A 'breezy' read is in store for anyone who gets past your cover page.

Excellent!

Here's something that you may not have taken into consideration.

Try not to leave any "hanging orphans" on your pages, either in the description or the dialogue areas. Yeah, hanging orphans -- or as I like to call them - nubs.

What in the hell is a nub?

It's a single word, at the end of a sentence, that's dangling all by its very lonesome self on its very own line of description or dialogue. Yup, just sitting there, all alone, where sometimes the reader doesn't even see it. And that can't be good. Nubs also tend to make your pages seem cluttered.

I have a pain in the ass screenwriting buddy of mine who is constantly harping on me about my hanging-orphan-fucking-nubs. But he's right (the sumbitch…).

Try going through your drafts right now and see how many nubs you have. I bet you'll have quite a few. If not, you're living the nub free dream. What a beautiful thing.

If you're not nub free, polish up those screenplays by editing, or expanding your descriptions and dialogue by a word or two (Note: For me, living nub-free usually involves editing words out of the pages rather than adding). Living nub free will make your pages appear even whiter, leaner, and 'breezier' than they are now. Your readers will thank you.

I can only hope now that all the nubs have been eliminated when this book was formatted and printed. I fear that they're here… lurking.

Chapter 44

From Scratch

Congratulations, you've completed the first draft of your latest screenplay. Go out and celebrate your accomplishment for now, because reality is about to rear its ugly head. Now it's time for the actual writing to begin -- The rewriting.

As you well, or should know, rewriting is a crucial part of the entire completed screenplay process. So why scrimp by not rewriting completely from the start? I'm talking to you, Mr./Ms./Mrs. writer who simply adds here and there, or cuts this or that, from the original first draft.

Here's what I do. I start completely over again from scratch.

Of course I use the original printed first draft as a guide for my second draft, but I actually rewrite/retype the entire screenplay from page one. This may not seem foreign to some of you (good for you!), but it is to several fledgling writers that I've met through the years.

Rewriting/retyping, from the start, from scratch, is important for one major reason. Your screenplay will be much, much better for the effort. Each word is reconsidered, each sentence mused over a second time, and dialogue is polished even further.

When you simply add/subtract from the original first draft, you'll begin to gloss over portions of your screenplay that may need work. Don't allow the old copy & paste and computer programming ease of use to curb your creativity. Sure it's easy to type over the existing text in your screenwriting program, but you're short changing the finished screenplay.

Rewriting is reworking. Reworking your screenplay makes for a more improved finished product.

You put so much time, creativity, and effort into completing your screenplay, so don't short shrift the final product. Go the extra "from scratch" mile. You'll notice the difference. And better yet, so will any potential readers.

Chapter 45

Wake Up

Would you like to garner an audible groan from a reader in Hollywood? Here's a surefire way to achieve that ill-fated goal. Write a dramatic screenplay with an outrageous, exciting, spectacular, over the top opening sequence, followed by the descriptive line—

'He wakes from the dream.'

You can almost hear the loser "Wah-Wah-Wah-Waaaaaah" music playing in the production offices around town after that "false start" screenplay is read.

And how do I know this? I fell into this trap early in my writing career. I also learned from that mistake and moved on, never again writing another "false start" opening. Please learn from my errors. Toss the "false starts!"

I'm talking dramatic screenplays, people, not comedy. A well crafted opening "dream sequence" could be quite effective in a comedy.

Here's the main problem with the dramatic "he wakes from the dream" scenario. Most of the time you're introducing the reader to this great character who's involved in some incredible action. Once the "dream" is revealed the character, often times, at least initially, in "real life," turns out to be an "every day" schlep with a boring existence. Boring life can equal boring character.

I'll let you in on a little secret. Boring doesn't sell. And it's your job to write the most saleable screenplay you can.

If you're writing for your own production and you're putting up the dough for the film, dream away, my friend. Otherwise, wake up, and lose the "dream" sequences at the very beginning of your screenplay.

And that's not to say your character, once he/she's established, can't delve into a dream sequence or two, no. It's just too dangerous to do from the very start. An opening dream sequence is a shoddy and fucking overused hack writer tactic.

Strive for "oohs" and "aahs" not "Wah-Wah-Waaaahs" from the Hollywood reader.

Wallflowers Need Not Apply
_____

Chapter 46

ComedyQuest

Good comedy is derived from drama. We usually laugh the hardest at situations that are based, solidly, in dramatic reality. Our brains understand that type of comedy because we've "been there." Example: It's 20 degrees below zero, you're driving from Wisconsin to Iowa. You stop for gas, leave your engine running, and yeah; you lock yourself out of your car. Hahahaha…ha…ha…ha… Okay, it happened to me.

So good comedy comes from drama, but be very careful not to delve too far, and too long, into the drama that created that comedy in the first place.

Let's say you have a character that is out to prove himself in the world. Nothing will get in his way, except maybe for himself. You show how driven he is, and you make his character development interesting and comedic. You may choose to delve just slightly into the serious side of what made him the way he is today.

The trick is to not stay with the serious side too long. Watch any of the classics by Lowell Ganz & Babaloo Mandel (*City Slickers, Parenthood, Night Shift, A League of Their Own*), and you'll quickly discover that the characters are driven by some fairly serious "stuff." But Ganz & Mandel rarely dip their creative toes into the serious pool for too long. And if they do it's through a mix of seriousness and comedy.

Here's a little trick that I developed for myself, and it's quite easy to do.

I map the comedy.

I will make a graph with the number of each page in my screenplay. I re-read my screenplay and next to each page number I place an E (Exposition), an F (Funny), or an S (Serious), based on what's on the page. After I "map" the screenplay, it just takes me one glance to see if there are too many S's in a row. And I really don't have to explain that too many S's in a row, in a comedy = not good.

I usually discover that some of the pages have all three letters showing, and that's not a bad thing. If you have too many E's by themselves, or, especially, too many S's in a row, you should rework the shit out of the screenplay. It is a comedy after all.

Take the time to map the comedy. Your screenplay will be stronger for it.

Chapter 47

Live It

Have you completed a screenplay or twenty without any of them being optioned or produced?

In my book, you're a screenwriter. Yes, like most screenwriters, you may still be on the upward climb to screenwriting competency, but you are actually completing screenplays, and that counts for something.

With any lifelong venture like screenwriting, or acting, or attempting to become an underwater explorer, you have to perform one major function day in and day out to achieve your life's dream.

You have to "live it."

You ARE a screenwriter. There's no need to shrink into the corner at parties because you haven't made a deal on any of your screenplays. How do you think produced writers get to that point in their careers? They told a lot of people that they're screenwriters. And with practice, they made sure that they told the right people, too. You may have a day gig as a realtor, or customer service rep, but when you're not answering to the man, or even when you are, you're a screenwriter. Let the world know.

"Be the screenwriter, Danny!"

Of course, someday you'll tell someone you've just met that you're a screenwriter and be thumped with the dreaded "Dude, have I got a story idea for you" scenario. You know, the situation where the person in question says they have the "bestest" idea ever, and if you write it, they'll gladly pay you a tiny percentage of whatever it makes. Yeah. Um, no.

It happens. It's happened to me – more than once (I didn't take the bait). But take the great with the not so good.

I was fortunate enough to meet a music business executive in Los Angeles several years ago who was a friend of a friend. When he asked what I did, I told him that I was a screenwriter. Cutting to the chase, shortly after, and directly connected to that first introduction, I was able to secure a screenwriting gig, and an agent. It does happen, folks.

Keep your external "is she/he in the business?" radar on and scanning at all times. You just never know whom you may be speaking with.

Make sure you're open to meeting and speaking with new people and telling them what you do, even when your confidence is waning. You may not directly be telling a Producer that you're a screenwriter, but you may be speaking with the Producer's brother.

If you're shy – as difficult as this can be - try and get over it (had a Dr. Phil moment, sorry). The "squeaky wheel rule" is definitely in effect, especially in the movie-making world.

Networking begets networking. What a beautiful thing. And so what if you're in Albuquerque and not Santa Monica? Producers are from all over. And most likely their families are back from where they came in the first place.

Here are a few methods I use for "living it": writing every day, whether it's note taking, actually writing/typing a screenplay, or simply daydreaming and noodling an idea over.

I read as many "first draft" screenplays that have been produced (not shooting scripts) that I can.

See movies – in the movie theater!

You can also check the Internet for screenwriter's blogs. There are many out there, and most of these seasoned vets offer some great advice.

Try to keep track of screenplay sales, what's selling, and why. Read as many screenwriting articles, and interviews, as you can.

When you "live it" you always run the risk of getting the old "Uh, oh, I'm stuck with the dreamer" eye roll from your friends and loved ones. Do what I did -- get new loved ones.

I kid!

You know that your nearest and dearest are only trying to look out for your best interests. However, I'd put good money on wagering that most of the non-writers in your life just don't seem to understand what drives you toward this vocation. Hell, I don't even know why I write. Simply make sure you're also striving for some sort of balance in your personal life, and live it!

Chapter 48

Market Wise

This may not be a very popular chapter with some of you, especially the artsy types. And I really can't apologize in advance because, well, this is mostly the way things work in the screenwriting game - especially the Hollywood spec screenwriting world.

Hopefully this is a no-brainer for the vast majority of you.

If you're trying to break into screenwriting (Hollywood style), and you're going to take the time and effort to craft an interesting screenplay, you better make sure that your idea is marketable.

Marketable? How?

Well, is there a lot at stake for your characters? Will your audience stay entertained by the progression of the story? (As they say, 'just cause it happened to you, doesn't necessarily make it interesting') Is the screenplay visually appealing? Are we entering into new facets of life we've never experienced before? Have you placed an original spin on the story?

Yes, there are a lot of interesting subjects you can write about that are not really "commercial," or that have fantastic "marketing hooks." Of course there have been numerous films made that, on the surface, don't seem marketable, that have gone on to do quite well. But...

The folks in charge in Hollywood, generally speaking, would rather see your spec writing efforts be spent crafting something that they can sell. And this means a story that's both gripping and can be described in the fewest words possible. And if they cannot buy completely into your screenplay writing style, they can at least see that your thought process is skewing toward "marketable."

Make sure that the initial log line you write before diving into the actual scripting of your screenplay jumps off the page. Try it out on people you know, especially people who aren't that crazy about you. Because if they like the idea and it sounds like something they'd pay to see, then you may be onto to something.

Yeah, yeah, "commercial" and "marketable" are so subjective. But are they?

Again – go back to your log line. If the screenplay can be described in one sentence (or so), and it stirs emotion in the reader, you may be looking at a marketable idea and something a Producer may purchase.

I'm not saying the story idea has to be too simplistic, it just has to pop. In fact, a simple one-sentence log line could quite easily wind up being a very complex and riveting screenplay.

The film *Fight Club* comes to mind. Log line: An office employee

Wallflowers Need Not Apply

and a soap salesman build a global organization to help vent male aggression.

The film has a great title and a very simple log line, which evokes enough curiosity that our imaginations are open to all sorts of possibilities. The film made nearly $110 million dollars.

Yes, I know it was based on a book, and yes having Brad Pitt in your film can't hurt, but they had to lure Pitt into the fold somehow, right? You think it was the initial story line, and secondly the screenplay, that attracted the talent?

The basic story line is what will always get you in the door; the quality of the screenplay will (hopefully) keep you there.

Even a well-crafted story line alone can sometimes (if you're a working pro but this is nearly impossible for a new writer) get you a deal. Maybe the screenplay can't back up that initial killer story line, but the story is strong enough for a Producer to buy it up and have it reworked into the product they want to sell. It does happen.

Marketable story lines rule the day in Hollywood, whether you like hearing that or not.

If you're not enamored with the "system," I suggest one thing. And I'm not being snide, snarky, or condescending…

Produce your own films. Show the world that you can make films that are both "non-mainstream" and can earn money at the box office, because inevitably, in this business, it'll always come down to making money for a Producer and/or an investor (s). Plain and simple.

In Hollywood they don't call it "Show Art" – it's known as Show Business...

Chapter 49

You're Gonna Make It

Several years ago, I was approached to do a seminar on low budget film making during a writers conference being put together by a screenwriting organization in LA. There were approximately 300 people in attendance at the writer's conference that year, and I had about 50 of the attendees in a conference room early on a Saturday morning. A very famous writing coach and script consultant was in the next room with the remainder of the folks at the conference, all 250 of them.

As I was about to begin the session, in walked the famous writing dude. Into my room! He was letting the 250 folks next door wait just a few extra minutes for his arrival. He walked straight up to me and introduced himself, leaned in close and whispered something to the effect of, 'I wanted to let you know that I'll be next door kicking your ass.' I laughed, because I knew he was being facetious.

The famous writing coach was disappointed that the folks at the conference couldn't attend both of the seminars, but with scheduling, time restraints, etc., it was impossible.

He went on to explain that he thought the 250 people waiting next door may be better served in my session. He basically said that working toward getting screenplays written and sold is a fantastic journey to take on, but writing and trying to make your own films and becoming a filmmaker is another solid path to "breaking in."

For the record, I do both. I write higher budget screenplays that I can sell through my agent, and produce my own Indie films. Having lots of 'irons in the coals' is a great thing.

Okay, so you're going to write, possibly direct, and certainly keep your hand in the producing side of getting your screenplay independently filmed.

Hopefully you have a way to raise all, or at least some, of the production money (I'm not going to get into fundraising/distribution here – another time, maybe).

So...You're the Producer, maybe director, too, so you don't have to worry about having your screenplay really looking like a screenplay, right?

Hey, it's just you and a bunch of people, most likely your friends, having fun and making an Indie movie. Hell, you can hand scribble the screenplay on crumpled 'In and Out Burger' bags if you want to.

And if you do, you'd be making a huge fucking mistake.

I'm going to go out on a limb and guess that you don't have more than a few million dollars in the bank to cover your production expenses. If you're like most Indie filmmakers, you have barely

Wallflowers Need Not Apply

enough to cover pizza, granola bar, and generic bottled water costs (I still have cases left over from my last production).

You, of course, want your movie to have some degree of success but you don't have the big dollars for production, however you hopefully do have the guts to approach, and attract some "name" or "face" talent to your film and win them over with a compelling story. That "name" can possibly bring distribution and success.

Define "name/face?" Sure, any excellent actor who has a recognizable face as well as some monetary/and/or critical success/acclaim from the films they've worked on.

You probably won't get an A-List actor to do your movie, but you could possibly attract any of the vast number of non-A List actors that are out there - ones who need work.

How do you get to these excellent, well known, actors? Do what I do when trying to put Indie productions together. I call them - on the phone. No wallflowers, remember?

Some of these actors represent themselves. Or you can go through their agents or managers. You can find actors contact information by calling the SAG offices in LA or by subscribing to a service like ImdbPro.com (I'm still not a paid endorser…I definitely have to work on that…).

So you've made the initial contact, pitched your story, and received a very positive response. Along with a 'yeah, send the screenplay' from the actor or their representative. All right, how do you seal the deal of getting the actor to come aboard and to begin negotiating a deal?

You make damn sure that your screenplay is in the exact same polished condition it would be in if you were to send it out to Producers or Production Companies. Your screenplay has to shine to attract potential investors, the crew, and especially that "name."

You probably won't be able to use the old 'I'm directing, so I really don't need the actors to know what's going on' excuse. So make sure that your screenplay is well written and within the appropriate page length parameters (90 to 120), and properly formatted. You'll hopefully be dispensing the screenplay to professional actors and crew so make sure it looks the part. They'll expect no less.

I know there may be some of you wondering why I even wrote this chapter. "Of course I want my best stuff sent out." But you would be amazed (!) at how many times I've been confronted by the scenario laid out here from other writer/producer/directors. That, to me, is amazing (The shitty kind of amazing).

Don't get caught in the "Screenplay, I don't need no stinking screenplay" scenario, it could lead to an early demise for your project.

Wallflowers Need Not Apply

Chapter 50

Market Wise-Up

There will always be rule breakers that "win" in film-dom, the "little movies that could." The movies *My Big Fat Greek Wedding, Little Miss Sunshine,* and the incredible *The King's Speech* come to mind when mentioning this category.

Unfortunately, when you're writing specs for the "*Hollywood Producer*" you can't count on the "little movie that could" factor. You have to approach the Hollywood style spec writing process by eliminating any possible anti-marketing hurdles you can.

"So what if my story is a smaller budget film, it's an interesting character study, won't that sell?"

Sure…maybe…

I'm not advocating that you don't write to your passions when tackling your spec scripts. What I'm writing about is that to play in the world of Hollywood spec screenplay writing, you have to understand that your interesting character study, although well written, and fascinating, may not have the marketing legs a Producer is looking for. Smaller films with no marketing "hook" can be a tough sell in Hollywood. Can you add a marketable hook to your story without destroying it?

"What about word of mouth once my film is produced, aren't Producers interested in that?"

That's a nice thing for the audience to hear about, word of mouth. It makes us all warm and fuzzy thinking that we, the people, "found" this film and we, as a democratic film going audience, helped to make it successful. It's damn cool.

A Hollywood Producer looking at your screenplay doesn't want to risk having to rely on word of mouth. They LOVE when it happens, but they can't ever count on it.

In the Indie filmmaking world word of mouth can be crucial because the filmmakers most likely don't have the marketing budget to compete with the big guys, but to the Hollywood Producer who is bringing this project to a major studio or a major investor, they will try to abate any risk from the get go.

That means the Producer wants a marketable story that appeals to main demographics (16+ year old males). It has to be a project that he/she can attach stars to, with a top director, and maybe even a top cinematographer attached, as well.

As you probably already know, that's one of myriad reasons we see so many remakes and films produced from successful (key word here - successful!) novels, plays, graphic novels, comic books, video games, and TV shows. They have a built in audience and a great head start on marketing.

Of course, there are a lot of smaller interesting films out there.

Wallflowers Need Not Apply

But remember, most of them are not based on the sale of a spec screenplay. The smaller films are usually pet projects of movie industry pros (actors, directors, etc.). Or they're self or low budget funded and interesting enough for a decent distributor to pick up. Again, they are normally not the type of spec screenplays sold to Hollywood Producers.

Producers are in the business of protecting their jobs (I literally had a Producer say that to me, verbatim, a few weeks ago). So, in essence, they will keep their jobs by saying no to you.

A Producer will only say yes to what they know they can sell. And that amounts to less than 1% of what's written. There are nearly 60,000 screenplays registered with the WGA, and only 300-400 major motion pictures produced in a given year. And those registration numbers don't reflect the screenplays that are only registered to the Library of Congress and not through the WGA.

We're all up against it.

If we're trying to play in the Hollywood spec screenwriting world, we have to really study that market, write to our passions, try to add interesting, and possibly marketable "hooks" to our story lines. We have to keep an eye on what will make money for a Producer and investors. This may sound crass to some of you (it does to me sometimes), but…

It's show business. Emphasis on business.

Chapter 51

Autobio-Dwell

You know that even established screenwriters write spec scripts. You already knew that, right? And there is a singular quality that every successful screenwriter I've ever met possesses.

Once they think their latest project is ready for others to read (and I know this can be the scary part), they let them go, kick them out of the nest.

They write, complete the spec screenplay, and basically move on. I'm not saying they gloss over the writing process, or scrimp on their research and prep time - nope.

It just seems that they know when it's time to move on to the next thing. Some of these writers have written 20, 30, 40 spec scripts over their careers, with just a fraction having been optioned/and/or/sold/and/or/produced.

Waiting can be death to the screenwriter's career. Keep creating!

Of course, the successful writer may come back to an earlier completed screenplay and rewrite, polish, etc., before resubmitting to Producers, but basically the produced writers I've met along the way, if they're not working on an assignment, all try to move on to the next spec project as soon as they can.

As the old adage goes – Writers write.

But some of the screenwriters I've met through the years seem to dwell too long on one singular project without creating anything new. And when I say dwell, I mean that they can spend years on one project, never writing anything else but that first, and only, screenplay -- Over and over and over again.

Unfortunately, I've seen a lot of this.

I'm not quite sure why this is, but the majority of the screenwriters I've met who "dwell" seem to be writing autobiographies. This got me wondering why they have such a difficult time finishing the screenplay (about themselves, of course) and moving on.

I have a theory. It may not be a very good theory, but here goes. I think it's because they cannot come up with a proper ending for their story, and they're stumped.

And do you know why that is? There is no "end" to them (I am not hoping for end to any of them…well most of 'em). How the heck are they supposed to end their screenplay if there is no "end" to them?

Maybe all the guessing on how their story should conclude keeps them from completing the screenplay, and the endless cycle of writing and rewriting that one singular screenplay continues.

Quite the quandary, isn't it?

There's also that pesky problem of having details in their lives change from time to time, so the screenplay has to reflect those changes, as well.

Well, that's my half-baked theory…

I was recently having my hair cut and the nice woman working her magic on my (lack of) mane knows that I'm a writer. She said, "I forgot to tell you that my brother-in-law writes screenplays."

Cool!

But then she went on, "Well, he's written one. And for the last 6 years he's kept writing it over and over again."

"I bet the story is about him."

"Do you know my brother-in-law?!"

No, not really. But, unfortunately, I do know him in a way.

Write your screenplay to its polished best, and move on to the next project. More "irons in the coals," means more chances of success.

Chapter 52

Voice

Have you had someone who's read your screenplays say, "You have to find your voice?" Or, "I'm not buying into your voice?"

It's such an ethereal notion, this "voice." What does it really mean?

When a reader isn't buying your "voice," it usually means that your writing style is useable at best, dry and boring at worst. You probably already guessed that that's not a good thing.

I had to write a few screenplays before I found my "voice" (cough-slow learner-cough).

To me, my "voice" is the way I try and make sure the reader is zipping quickly through my pages, while getting the most of my story line.

How do I accomplish this?

I make sure that all the various portions of my screenplays are fun to read. Page turners. Breezy. There should also be lots and lots of white space on the page. The word "breezy" is your friend when describing a screenplay. (Please refer back to the Blocky Description chapter)

We're not novelists! We don't have the luxury of delving into our character's heads for pages on end. We have to "show" what our characters are experiencing. And we have to set the story up quickly.

Using comedy as an example: I let my "voice" loose by basically having "jokes" and "pay offs" in the description portion of my screenplays. In a lot of cases my description is unfolding in the exact opposite way of what the character may be saying. That juxtaposition of events creates comedy on the page (hopefully transferring to the screen). What the character is actually saying may not necessarily be funny, but it is comical because we know, and "see," that everything is askew.

You can do the same with a drama. The character may be trying to be funny or nonchalant, but we know that the scene isn't, and that something dreadful may be happening soon.

"Voice" also comes into play with your timing. Like when and where to place a joke or a dramatic turn in your screenplay. Timing is difficult to teach, but with writing practice you can hone your timing skills.

What it really comes down to is using your personality to draw in a reader.

If you have a comedic personality, use it on the page. If you have a darker, more dramatic persona, make sure that it's reflected in your screenplays. Most of us, fortunately, have a little of both.

Wallflowers Need Not Apply

This may seem counter-intuitive, but another way to establish your "voice" is to not have your characters talk so much. They're movies, moving pictures, not "talkies." Some of the most memorable characters in cinema rarely speak, and when they do, we damn sure listen. And the most compelling characters in film are mostly involved in some incredible action. Have the character speak through their actions.

Use your writers "voice" to draw in the reader, your first audience, to the world you've created. Keep them there with crisp, enjoyable description, and snappy dialogue.

Your "voice" is in there, you know it is. See how other writers demonstrate their "voice." Read "first draft" screenplays that have ultimately been produced (not shooting scripts! Read first drafts!). You can find several, free of charge, online.

Experiment by using an economy of descriptive words to tell your story. Have fun with your pages. Utilize lots of white space and make sure your screenplays are enjoyable to read and page-turning wonders.

Chapter 53

Proper Groupings

I think writing groups can be invaluable, for a time, anyway. Until a group member personally disses another's writing prowess and a literary free-for-all erupts. It's a common occurrence.

Okay, confession time. I rarely, if ever, allow anyone outside of my inner circle of a few trusted readers to look at my screenplays before they head out to Producers. Why? Because I'm a big baby!

Not really.

I've discovered through the years that the more folks I had read my work, the more opinions I got. That obviously makes sense. But all of those opinions were sometimes confusing and contradictory. What you find yourself in is a sort of development scenario. And it's a development "deal" that you're not getting paid for.

Sometimes you just have to go with your gut and a few well placed, and trusted, readers to make sure you're on target or not. If that's accomplished through a writer's group – Cool!

Wallflowers Need Not Apply

I had the pleasure of being a panelist at a big film festival in Texas a few years back. During some down time I sat in on a panel being headlined by one of the superstar screenwriters responsible for a whole series of pirate flicks. The man is an incredible screenwriter, and a good guy, too. Someone asked him about writing groups and he seemed to agree with my previous thoughts. But then he went a bit further.

He said he belongs to a small filmmaking group, not a writing group. He and a select few of his friends, people he trusts implicitly, gather to write and read 5 page short screenplays that they've created. Each time they meet, a different short is chosen and filmed. One group member owns a camera, another lighting equipment, etc., etc. (and I bet they can land a few "decent" actors along the way).

Why did they form a filmmaking group? Mister superstar screenwriter dude and his friends realize that writing a screenplay and making a film of that screenplay are two VERY different things. Your words on paper can have a different meaning/feel when spoken/acted, often times not to the hoped for result. Things will change from paper to actor, actor to camera, and camera to editing process.

The superstar screenwriter explained that the screenwriting filmmakers in his group work out writing kinks by seeing their work in action, without the great expense of shooting a feature film.

Genius!

They become even stronger screenwriters by filming, and seeing their work in action. This is excellent advice.

Another way to accomplish seeing your work play out - pun intended - as a writing group or solo is to partner with a local theater group. Simply devise a plan where you write a short piece and allow the actors to do their thing on stage. You can find holes in your writing, and the actors can, well, act! It's a win-win. And the costs should be minimal. This approach, of course, is best used for working on dialogue.

I'd suggest keeping your writing group size small, or to have break out groups to limit the exposure of your screenplays to so many opinions, especially in some of the larger groups (more than 20). Try to keep all the opinions in perspective. The folks in the group are there to help, not come down on you (I'd hope). Thick skin is a prerequisite for anyone venturing into the screenwriting world. Take it all in, listen; try not to be defensive, because the group members may be onto something that you never considered being a problem in the past.

It's not easy sitting back and taking the criticism, but it can be quite beneficial to your finished screenplay.

There's something ingrained in the excellent screenwriters I've met that tells them that they're on track as far as their ideas/writing/execution, so you also have to let your gut guide you.

Listen and take in the criticism, but of course keep to your personal standards and tastes. You'll know soon enough if you're on track, especially after a few professional Producers take reads and like what they're seeing. If you're getting the opposite result or no responses at all on your work from professionals, it's probably time to take a different approach with your writing.

Let me end by saying that the writer's groups that I am familiar

Wallflowers Need Not Apply

with all seem to be going after one singular achievement. They all want each and every member of their group to succeed (when they're not trying to kill one another).

Chapter 54

No Time Like The Present

There may be a few spec screenwriters out there that are going to dislike reading this. I say to you - tough shit.

Writing and selling specs is difficult enough as it is. Selling a period piece spec screenplay is even more so.

For those who are not familiar, period pieces are described as screenplays set in the past. Sci-fi is basically considered a futuristic period piece. So, quite simply, any story not based in present day (give or take a few years).

I know, I know – you have all the cool old buildings, vintage cars, and wardrobe. And don't get me started on Sci-Fi and CGI.

"Why are period pieces so difficult to sell?"

Simple. If done correctly, they're usually very expensive to produce. If done poorly they end up looking like shit.

You know how much it costs to get those old buildings, cars, wardrobes, or futuristic special effects? You can bet that it's a lot more in production dollars than filming something "present day."

"But why do we see period piece films hit the theaters every year?"

Most often, they're not based on spec screenplay sales. Most have been in the works for years (assignments, etc.) through Production Companies and Studios. A lot of them are pet projects of established industry professionals. And most futuristic period pieces are based on well-known, and successful (key word), comic books, graphic novels, and video games. Producers rarely take the chance of sinking millions of dollars into a production written by a Newbie. Sure it happens – just not that often. Knowing all of this, why would you mess with your chances of actually selling your spec by writing a period piece?

Now, all that being typed, if you go into the spec screenwriting process knowing your period piece will be a very tough sell, but you're damn sure it'll be an excellent way of showcasing your writing skills – write it!

Just realize going in that it's a more difficult, not impossible, sell job than writing a "present day" spec screenplay.

Chapter 55

Screenwriting Biz 101

"What do you think about people who don't take the time to learn the business? People who read one book or attend one seminar and don't want to listen to anything or anyone else because they now think they know everything there is about screenwriting?"

No one knows it all. Your education should be ongoing.

(I'm going to write to the screenwriting world, but the following should, of course, hold true for any business you're trying to break into.)

Listen to as many working experts (not the people who simply tell you that they're experts, but the people who have actually done the work) as you possibly can, through seminars, books, interviews, etc. Learn to take it all in without trying to spout your new rules before you even learn how to utilize the old ones first. The working experts have been there, so learn from their success (and their mistakes). Get as many points of view as you can. I think you should be constantly on the lookout for what working experts are saying.

Wallflowers Need Not Apply

I've been writing screenplays for several years, have made numerous deals, I have an agent, had Indie films produced, etc. I still feel like a lost and lonely screenwriter in the woods sometimes. I am always looking for new information, direction, and advice.

I know most new writers have day gigs, but even so, if you're not attacking your screenwriting career full out, with the time you have available to you, you're missing the boat. Of course it's perfectly fine to be a "hobbyist" in the screenwriting world, but it'll be nearly impossible for you to ever have success if this is only a sideline for you.

Screenwriting in either the Indie or Hollywood arenas can be a full-contact sport. The competition is fierce, so why would you want to shortchange yourself? Get as much screenwriting information into your head as possible, and draw on that information as you complete screenplays.

This should all sound like a no-brainer to you, but you'd be AMAZED at how many new writers assume that because they've been in the audience at a movie theater that they can write, and produce, a film.

If you were trying out for an NFL team as a free agent, would you know all there is about making the team because you've seen a few games on TV? On top of having natural talent, I would hope that you'd try to be in the best shape of your life, and know the game. You'd probably already have high school and hopefully college football experience, right? The same holds true for screenwriting. You'll want to get into the best possible shape by learning the craft. It can be very time consuming, but at least you're giving yourself a shot at the big time.

Chapter 56

A Closer Look At Book Rights

"How do I get the rights to a book in order to write a screenplay based on the work?"

Cash – lots and lots of cash.

Most, if not all, major publishing deals these days involve the film rights being negotiated from the start. So if you're trying to option a current New York Times Best Seller, your chances of landing the property are VERY slim. The film rights are probably already wrapped up. But if you have lots-o-dough to negotiate a deal where you purchase the rights away from the current holder, you may be on your way. (Hey, there may be some readers out there with that kind of cabbage, right? Hello?).

Here's another way of approaching the 'securing film rights' quandary -- The no to low budget way.

Locate books that have had some succes but may be out of the popularity loop at present. Don't get me wrong, the rights to these books are probably already wrapped up, too, but the rights holder may be willing to hear your passionate pitch (key phrase) on why you want the rights and just HAVE to write the screenplay and get the film produced.

Your passion for the book could wind up being your currency for securing the rights. Having passion for projects is your friend, especially when you don't have money.

Important note – Make sure that the book your trying to get the rights to has had some success. It doesn't necessarily have to be a former New York Times Best Seller (although this is a good thing), but a piece that has some sort of following. Having a built in audience will heighten your chances of making a deal down the road with a Production Company, or with a distributor if you plan on producing the film yourself.

I've actually optioned a book in the past. It was an older and VERY successful book. I was able to negotiate a very small option price for a one-year option. Long story short, I couldn't get any larger Production Companies to bite. The option was up, and I moved on. The publisher was interested in my pitch because I was - you guessed it – very passionate about the project. If you haven't already, you'll learn soon enough that a good number of the projects you'll try to get off the ground don't pan out. It's the nature of the business.

What about optioning someone's true-life story?

This can be a little easier, especially if the story is incredible, but not highly publicized. Find a way to get in direct contact with the person (s) involved in the real story and simply negotiate some sort of deal with them. Again, show your zeal for the project. You may want to also get an entertainment attorney involved at this point. There can be rights issues if you're utilizing a newspaper or magazine article for your source information. The original news writer may frown on you taking their angle and making it into "your story." I'd advise that you contact a lawyer (CYA). You can also negotiate a deal where the lawyer works on deferment and is paid if you can set the deal up somewhere. I've worked deals like this in the past. Passion can be a powerful currency.

Here's something to keep in mind, though. If your passion gets you in the door and the rights holder is willing to work a low or no money deal with you, don't expect to have a lot of time to A) write the screenplay, and B) to set up a deal somewhere with the property. Generally speaking, no money, or low money = smaller option time period. More money = more time to write and set up a deal.

Chapter 57

Network!!!

"Can you get me an agent?"

"Can you get me the phone number to Steven Spielberg's office?"

No. And I have actually received these types of questions more than once.

Why a "no?"

Firstly, I don't have Spielberg's number. I have never met the man, although I hear that he's a fantastic guy.

Secondly, go out and find your own agent. I did. It took a lot of persistence and work, but finally I was able to achieve that seemingly lofty goal through networking.

You're going to soon discover that just because you have an agent you're not going to stop "selling" yourself, or sit back and allow your agent to do all the heavy lifting. For me, just

Wallflowers Need Not Apply

the opposite applies. My agent is simply another member of the team, and together, we will conquer the world! Cough-cough… sorry…

Whenever anyone asks me something like the dreaded 'do you know Spielberg' question, I always laugh at the memory of watching the Albert Brooks film *The Muse*. In the movie, Brooks' character is a struggling writer with a bad case of writer's block. He finally lands a meeting with "S. Spielberg" at DreamWorks, only to discover his long awaited meeting is with Stan Spielberg, Steven's third cousin.

So, sorry, I'm not going to offer you up names of agents I know, or numbers for top notch industry pros that I may or may not even know.

But I will offer this to you. Whether you live in LA or not, and you want a chance to make it in the movie business, learn all that you can about the business, and -- Network!

Network, network, network – and network some more. It is what you know, coupled with who you know. "Hollywood" is like any other industry. Know what you're doing and meet people who would like to work with you. If you're looking for info about truck driving jobs wouldn't you ask around to your friends and family to see if any of them know truck drivers? Why act differently because you're trying to get a job in the film business? You're not asking for favors, you're seeking information about the business. Maybe a favor will come from the networking contact. Just don't ever count on it.

And if you can't find family or friends, or friends of friends of family members (huh?), begin your own network. Networks start somewhere…

Attend screenwriting, and filmmaking seminars. Join screenwriting and/or filmmaking groups. At seminars meet the working pros appearing on the panels. Buy them drinks, or ask them to lunch. Do whatever it takes to meet and greet the folks in the know. Make friends among the others who are trying to break in. One never knows where another will wind up a few years down the road. And you'll be making new friends with similar interests.

Here's a little trick that I sometimes do when meeting and getting to know new people. After starting a rapport with them, I'll call and say something like, "You know, I just finished writing a draft of my latest screenplay, and have some free time. Is there anything I can do for you or your company? Gratis."

You think I'm kidding? I do stuff like that all the time. I'm sincere in my offer, and I follow through, too. And you know what? People remember things like that. Go the extra networking mile. Make sure to keep in contact with your new network components, though. It takes time and effort to make contacts, try not to allow them to fade away.

If none of this has convinced you that networking is EXTREMELY important, consider this. At this writing I am currently under contract on two screenplay projects for a Production Company that's owned by a 32 year old man. This is the very same man that I met ten years ago when he was a 22 year old college student attending his first writer's conference.

Chapter 58

Psst, Buddy, Wanna Buy An Idea?

"I have a great story idea but I'm not a screenwriter. Will you pay me for my story idea and then write it yourself?"

Piss off.

Generally speaking, I think that ideas are a dime a dozen. It's the execution of said idea that will sell. So, asking for a payment for your idea is a little off-putting to most professional writers. They have enough ideas to last a writing lifetime (if not more).

Excellent Producers come up with ideas all the time, and guess what? They pay the screenwriter to write the idea for them. That's one of the main revenue sources for writers in the "Hollywood" system (assignments). Hopefully knowing that little bit of information will explain how, sorry, fucking stupid sounding that 'wanna buy my story' question will seem to a writer.

Here's the part where I tell you – "Learn the craft and write it yourself."

If you're able to come up with great ideas time and time again, maybe you should begin learning the craft of screenwriting and get after it. You may have some talent for this.

Chapter 59

The Real Writing Begins

"How do you attack rewrites?"

Great question!

And a difficult one to answer because I'm not sure I attack them all the same way. But here are some steps I use that hopefully can be of help to you as you start the real writing process - The rewriting.

(I'll speak to spec scripts because the assignments I've worked on are an entirely different, and time sensitive, process.)

I'm going to assume (dangerous sometimes, I know) that you've already mapped out your story by researching, creating characters, outlining, and that you have at least a first draft of the screenplay completed.

Heck, I'll actually start off by giving you (if you're interested) my initial writing process.

I'm one of those writers that research for quite some time, and "live" with the story through daily "noodling" sessions, where

I take copious notes. Most times I'll fill a couple of legal sized note pads with rambling scribbles. When I wrote a spec about SWAT teams I literally went out with a local SWAT team on an overnight training run. Ah, there's nothing like scrambling around in a bulletproof vest and being part of a live fire exercise. This "living with it" process will eventually become my outline, and of course, the first draft.

After my outline is set, and I'm primed to write, I---

Sorry, let me stop here...

"Primed to write?" What does that mean?

I don't know about you, but I have to live with the story running in my head for a time until, well, I just HAVE to write the first draft. It's almost as if my head will explode if I don't start writing. This pre-writing can sometimes take months. But once I begin writing the first draft, I usually complete it in about 3 or 4 days. Yeah, my ass is usually killing me from sitting for hours on end, but that's just the way I do things.

I write short first drafts, too (about 80 pages). I'm not one to write "long" and cut back (I went "long" with my notes). I get to the heart of the story in the first draft and create what I call "the bones" of the screenplay. In my first draft I may have what I call "place holder" scenes where I know I want something funny, dramatic, or whatever. I'll literally write a very brief scene, advancing the story while utilizing the characters and brief descriptions of the situations I want. I'll place just a bit of dialogue and description in those "placeholders" like "Something funny happens here," or "Emotional break through here."

Wallflowers Need Not Apply

I don't want to get bogged down with "perfection," so I make sure not to stop the story flow as I write that first draft. To me, I'd be completely stumped if I had to create the perfect scenes in my first draft. I simply churn through the first draft so I can get to Fade Out. It's a kind of race, or more accurately, a battle of wills – Me vs. "The Blank Page."

After I type Fade Out on that first draft, I usually print the screenplay and let it sit for a few days, maybe a week. I try not to think about it at all, which is kind of impossible, since I've been immersed in the story for so long. Instead I do stuff like Swiffer the floors for my wife.

When I come back to the screenplay, I read it over straight through. Then I reread it, and begin "pencil whipping" the pages, adding notes. I'll go back to my original notes and begin adding even more "meat" to those bones, hand written, and directly on the pages. Although not likely, I may even re-outline at this time. I try to have my story structured in the original outlining process, but sometimes things change, and I have to be able to "organically" go with the flow. I then sit with the pencil whipped first draft and erase the computer file of my original draft (yeah, scary, huh?), and literally rewrite the screenplay using the first draft pages as my guide.

Try this sometime. It makes you rethink every sentence of description, every bit of dialogue, because you have to literally type it over. There's no scrimping and scanning over the pages. I am truly rewriting the screenplay.

(House building analogy to follow – apologies in advance) For me rewriting is a layering process. First you're building a blueprint/foundation (original notes & outline). Then you work on the frame (the first draft). Soon you'll have a completed, but not quite decorated structure. That may come in the second, third, or fourth draft (or more). Through this rewriting process I'll have a trusted few readers take a gander and offer up notes. These notes usually don't literally make it into the next draft, but the reader's ideas usually get me rethinking scenes, etc., but in my own way, not necessarily theirs. Trusted readers are gold, especially ones that can spark your imagination.

I can quite comfortably state that I don't think any screenplay is actually ever finished.

You just have to trust your story telling and screenwriting instincts to let you know when to let the screenplay venture out into the cruel world. Even a completed screenplay is simply a blueprint to a film production. Things will change as directors and actors are added to the project.

And when filming begins, scenes will change on the spot (quite common). Even in the editing process, the original screenplay will change, especially when the director and editor need to trim scenes (also quite common). You may have heard this; 'A movie is written 3 times - Once as a screenplay, a second time during filming, and lastly in the editing process.'

Truer words.

Wallflowers Need Not Apply

Chapter 60

Floating Scripts

"How do you handle it when you send your script to a friend who is not in the biz and you want them to be careful not to let the script 'float' around?"

Dear paranoid person, there's an easy answer…

Don't send your shit to people not in, or trying to break into, the "biz." I'm sort of fucking with you – let me explain…

Here's a little something I've learned through the years. People not interested in screenwriting generally do not want to read your screenplay in the first place. They'd rather see the finished film. Okay, you're Mom may want to read it. But only if your Mom is the talented Paula Wagner, will it do you any good.

But think this one through - who are they going to show it to when they have finished reading that's going to go out and "steal" your screenplay idea? Chances are you're the only one they know who's a screenwriter. I think if you're going to ask someone to read a new piece of your work, and you're looking for honest feedback, the "trust factor" is implied, don't you?

If you can't trust the reader, maybe you're not paranoid, and you're sending the screenplay to the wrong person.

Hypothetical: What if (MAJOR what if!) the reader thinks that you're screenplay is so wonderful that they do "float" it to someone else, and so on and so on?

You could possibly have the screenplay float right into the hands of someone who can do you some good, a Producer, maybe?

Hey, a guy can dream, right?

And let's say you land an agent. What do you think that agent will be doing with your screenplay? Yeah, just a wee bit of "floating."

Wallflowers Need Not Apply

Chapter 61

Voices Of Screenplays Future

Here's an exercise for you to try as you rewrite or begin a new screenplay.

Pretend that the person who will eventually be reading your screenplay (either a professional reader or competition reader) doesn't know a damn thing about screenwriting. Nothing! Imagine that they couldn't tell a plot point from a cemetery plot, and that they wouldn't know a McKee from a McNugget, etc., etc.

You've crafted a great story line, created interesting characters, and structured your screenplay to perfection. Now you want to have a chance at it hovering to the top of this Newbie reader's "consider" list, right? (This applies to screenwriting contests, too)

Here's what you do. Make sure that your unique "voice" is prevalent throughout your entire screenplay. Even if the reader doesn't know much about the craft of screenwriting, they should be able to discern your "voice" from all the other shit they're reading. Hopefully you'll be able to entertain and draw them into your screenplay and keep them turning those pages. That is job #1 for screenwriters!

Pretty much anyone can write a banal, bland, boring, technical, and dry screenplay. But only you can add your distinctive "voice" to the work. Pump up the descriptions using an economy of expressive words. Make sure your comedic/dramatic timing is there (tough one to learn, but with practice, you can get better and better at it). You can be quite descriptive without being novelistic, you know. It is possible. I'm not talking about writing huge, bulky, passages of description. I repeat -- Use an economy of descriptive words.

"But you can't write too descriptively because the actors and director may frown on you for doing their jobs."

Fuck that noise!

Your job is to suck the reader into the story and keep them there. The reader is your audience! Your job is to "sell" the reader on the idea of passing your screenplay up the chain of command or onto the next round of a competition – and so on and so on. You MUST do this by exhibiting your "voice." Once the screenplay is sold, the actors and directors will do as they may with your work (and they will because that's the nature of the business). Your job is to get them all to that point in the process. And it's never going to happen with a blandly written piece of work because you'll be tossed out before that happens.

I'm sure this may all sound pretty obvious to some of you, but, the message isn't getting through.

Over the years, I've read in the neighborhood of 1,500

Wallflowers Need Not Apply

screenplays (for professionals and aspiring writers), and the one and only thing that will get, and hold, my attention – and will actually allow me to get into, through, and understand your story is – your unique "voice."

For me, "voice" equates to tone, timing, and the distinctiveness of descriptions.

And even if the reader doesn't buy into your story idea, they can definitely buy into your writing style, your "voice." That can possibly equate to an assignment, and it's all about getting work, right? Right!

Chapter 62

Consultations

Should you pay for a script consultant to review your work?

Okay, I feel like I've been caught with my pants down, and it is a liiitttttle breezy today. You see, I've never paid for a consultant to read my work.

Through dumb luck, networking, and sheer persistence, I've always been able to get my work into the hands of industry professionals, people who are actually making decisions, and movies. This little bit of blind-stupid-dumb-fucking luck, well, most times, supplied me with "free consultations," if you will.

Seriously, now -- Do I believe in consultants?

Yes, I do – sort of.

But with this caveat; make sure to do a little due diligence on the consultant to make sure they are for real. Anyone can hang the old consultant shingle out and charge a shitload to give you "guidance." There are a lot of assholes out there saying that they're experts who are not. Search for rankings and recommendations on consultants through reputable screenwriting sources (magazines, web sites, screenwriting organizations, etc) before making your decision.

And note – I'm not charging for this "consultation." Sort of…

Chapter 63

Screenwriting Contests: Yes or No?

Most screenwriting contests, with the exception of a very select few, are worthless. Here's a direct quote from an unnamed Producer friend of mine, "Winning a screenplay competition means only that you are the best of the worst writers."

I know there are a few "competitions" out there, if they're still in business (and contests are businesses) that have so many categories, and categories within categories, that nearly everyone who enters the contests "wins." That's sort of like having each and every little 5-year-old player in a soccer league snagging a trophy after the last match of the season.

If you are going to go the competition route, though, confirm that the contest you're entering is reputable and that there's a decent cash prize (I'd say a grand prize of $10,000 or more should suffice). The money is a surefire way to confirm that you're definitely benefiting from entering, and winning, the contest.

In addition to a nice cash prize, try to ensure that the contest is attempting to get you in front of real professionals who can perhaps further your career (if not directly from your winning screenplay, possibly with your unique writing style/voice).

Generally speaking, the winning competition screenplays are not what "Hollywood" is looking to produce (with the exception of the fantastic Nicholl Fellowship). Most winning competition screenplays are smaller, character driven stories. That's not a bad thing, but it's not what "Hollywood" is seeking for the most part. But winning a reputable contest could possibly get you enough notice to launch a career. Not likely, but maybe...

And that ten grand or more could go a long way toward paying off those credit card debts.

Chapter 64

What If?

Getting and keeping a foothold in this business, at least for me, has been a numbers game. You have to be working several projects at once to raise your chances of success. Right now I'm juggling several projects (options, an assignment, currently spec writing, and Indie producing).

With that in mind, do you ever put time aside so that you can conjure up new story ideas/log lines? Or do you simply wait for divine inspiration to strike and the stories to pop into your head? Your excellent writing skills can bring notice, but your capacity to constantly come up with great ideas can be the icing on the cake to a great career.

Here's something I do (you may be doing this, too) to keep after the ABC's (Always Be Creating). I take time out every month or so to sit with a legal pad & pen and come up with "What ifs/ and thens."

What's a "What if/and then?"

It's a simplistic way to create high concept ideas. Example: What if an aardvark is accidentally exposed to radioactive material, and then develops the skill sets to become a US Senator? (Okay a shitty example but hopefully you get the idea).

When I get into a story creating session, I usually crank some music (as always), sit outside, take in the views, and just let my mind wander. I try to match up two of the craziest story elements that I can to see if I can create a compelling "What if/And then" scenario. Crazy elements? Yeah, I try and come up with topsy-turvy ideas, matching the most unlikely people with the equally most unlikely circumstances. For me this works for both comedy and drama. You'll be amazed at the ideas you'll come up with.

Chapter 65

And The Protagonist Is?

"Is it a good idea to not introduce your protagonist until you're 25 pages into your screenplay?"

The short answer: Fuck no.

Now, if your protagonist is not seen, but spoken of, from the very beginning, and the character is set up so that we cannot wait (!) to finally meet him/her, that could possibly (possibly!) work. I think you're treading dangerous waters trying that angle, especially if you're early into a burgeoning career. But I could be wrong (I'm not).

I'd say that the majority of your audience members would want to meet the Protagonist as soon as possible so they know who they'll be rooting for. I think you'll confuse them if they're following one character, believing them to be the Protagonist, and then suddenly change focus to a new character, and then that character becomes the true Protagonist. It's actually confusing just writing about it…

I know it could be super cool to be "different" and carve new paths

Wallflowers Need Not Apply

for story telling/screenwriting, but the reality is that audiences are VERY intelligent. They've arrived at unconsciously knowing the structure of storytelling. This is nothing new. It's ingrained in their minds. Mankind has been telling/hearing stories since the beginning of time. The audience knows what's working and what's not. And the audience can usually tell when things are out of whack.

Writing a screenplay is like building a table. All the tables that people build will probably look different, but they have to stand up. That's structure. If you're not introducing your main character until almost 30 minutes into the film, you're structure will, most likely, be out of whack and your story will fall (down) apart. I'm sure there are examples to the contrary, but not too many.

Chapter 66

To Montage, Or Not To Montage

I like montages, especially in comedy.

When I'm watching a comedy and the main character(s) is plotting revenge, a comeback, etc, the time compression element of a good montage allows me to quickly get into the scene and wonder what's going to happen next. If the montage is a "tease" and doesn't allow me to see all that is being planned, the big reveal later in the movie of the montage "activities" can be rewarding, if done well.

I've written comedies in the past where I'll place a bit of contradictory voice over within the montage. So you have some outrageous stuff going on visually, but the Protagonist is verbally telling a completely different story. That same sort of juxtaposition can be accomplished by having two separate montages, one for the Protagonist, and one for the Antagonist playing in a cross-cutting manner. It's kind of like watching a chess match, not knowing exactly who will make the next move, and what that move may be.

Are montages overdone?

Wallflowers Need Not Apply

Maybe…

I also like to think that a montage is an effective filmmaking tool that audiences have come to accept, possibly even look forward to.

Please allow me to explain…

I like to see movies in the theater, and if I see one that I really like, I'll go back and see it yet again. On that second trip to the local theater, a lot of times, I'll watch the theater audience's reaction to portions of the movie. Okay, all right, I'm not a voyeur because it's for research, people. Really!

Anyway…

I gauge how the audience reacts to see if they respond the same way I did when I first watched the film. And for whatever reason, I've discovered that the second a montage starts, the audience will begin to smile, and maybe even laugh out loud. It's almost as if they're expecting it, but it's a familiar filmmaking "friend" they're happy to welcome into the theater and their hearts.

I don't know about you, but if you're consistently seeing positive audience reactions to montages, a montage may be something for you to explore for your next screenplay.

Chapter 67

Thick Skin

I had a nice conversation with a fledgling screenwriter from the Vancouver, BC area recently.

This guy was admittedly a lost babe in the woods when it came to even beginning the process of attacking a screenplay, but he was reaching out for information. He had the guts and the tenacity to track me down so he could get what little nuggets of information he could.

He was no nonsense, straight forward, and sounded like a solid guy. And you know what? He may possibly have a shot at this thing of ours.

Why?

One reason - He already has a nice layer of "thick skin."

Thick skin is a prerequisite for the screenwriter, because, man-o-man, you're going to be up against the wall the entire time you're tackling this career. You don't want to venture into a screenwriting career while trying to ignore the fact that it's a

Wallflowers Need Not Apply

difficult, DIFFICULT, journey, do you?

Head in sand = not good for chances at success.

I don't like to sugarcoat too much. If asked a direct question, I answer as directly as possible without too much bullshit. When prompted, I explained to my Canadian friend that he's got a tough road ahead. He was actually appreciative of the "non-tooth-achingly-sugarcoated" advice. That's the minute I knew he had thick skin.

Don't get me wrong, I don't want to dissuade any one from following a dream, just to be aware of the obstacles that lie ahead as they chase said dream. This British Columbia Newbie knew what he was up against and was still charging forward. Excellent! Love to see that.

Here's a brief description of a screenwriting career: When you think you have things firmly in control, you'll soon find yourself on your ass wondering what in the fuck happened to you.

The Chinese have a saying that relates to thick skin and tough tasks ahead: "Fall seven times, stand eight."

Yeah, you got it, get up and keep going. Thick skin. If you don't have it, acquire it - Quickly. And don't allow syrupy screenwriting experts to guide you down the wrong path. Screenwriting ain't easy at all. Know what you're up against. Learn as much as you can about the film industry, not just screenwriting. Know the odds. Learn how others got to where they are now, which paths to success they chose, etc., etc., etc.

And if you desire to move forward, and I HOPE you do,

completing and marketing screenplays can be a very rewarding venture.

Wallflowers Need Not Apply

Chapter 68

It's A Brevity Thing, Man

Having trouble getting Producers/Production Companies/agents/managers to read your screenplay? You've emailed, mailed, and phoned in queries to the above without any takers?

Getting anyone to read your work is as much a numbers game as it is a "do you have any talent" game. But it can be a numbers game with a twist.

I'm going to assume that you're not residing in the greater LA or NYC areas. Yeah, that can be a stroke against you, but it shouldn't be a complete stopper. Plenty of people from all around the world are getting reads in, say, Hollywood. But how did they get in and not you?

It may be your approach.

Make sure that your initial pitch to agents, and Producers, etc., are-- Wait a second. Let me stop for just a moment.

Forget about approaching agents.

I'll make your life a little less cluttered. Only go after Producers and Production Companies. You'll be going right to the source of a possible sale, and cutting out the middle man/woman from the get go. If your screenplay is snapped up, you'll find an agent, or better yet, they may find you. And you'll save 10% on that first deal, too.

Here's what you do. Get a copy of the Hollywood Creative Directory (available online as well), or a subscription to ImdbPro.com, or some other type of service, and – be your own agent.

You'll be able to research films similar to your screenplay that have been produced and find the contact information for the people and companies who produced those films. (Note: you may want to find companies that have made SUCCESSFUL films that are similar to yours). Some of these people and companies may be open to reading your query. Some of these Production Companies may require that you have some sort of representation. If that's the case pay a lawyer to be "your representative" and have them send queries on their letter head. You may even have a lawyer buddy who'd do that service for free (networking!).

Here's the twist to the numbers game, though. I'd recommend a focused attack. Don't shotgun your queries to every Production Company in town. Companies that usually produce horror films won't want to look at your *Bridgette Jones* re-hash. Do your research and know about the people you're sending the query to. If you send out queries to say 10 companies and get all "nos," refocus your attack, do some more research and get ready to send out the next wave of 10, and so on, and so on. Start with the top tier contacts and then work your way to the rest (if applicable). And make sure to follow up if you've not received a response. A month is a decent amount of time to wait.

Okay, now back to the actual query…

Make sure that your initial attacks (yes, "attack" seems like an appropriate word here) to Producers/Production Companies are brief, thought provoking, brief, descriptive, brief, something they can "see," and yes, brief. Hopefully you're into the "whole brevity thing," because being brief and descriptive can translate to you actually being a decent screenwriter. If your query is more than a paragraph or three, rewrite it. Brevity! The folks you're contacting have very little time. Approach the process as if you're writing a 15 second TV spot for your film. Yeah, it's marketing time! Get them to say yes with the fewest words you can. If you have more to say, say it after they've read your screenplay and want to meet with you.

If you're going on and on in your queries, and not much is really being said, well, the reader may assume that your screenwriting style is the same. That could translate to an immediate "no."

I'm not a big fan of "marketing tricks" to get people to read screenplays, but if it works for you, do it. There are no rules to how your "15 second TV spot" should appear. I have a screenwriting friend who wrote a comedic screenplay about construction workers. He Fedexed query letter wrapped bricks to Production Companies. It worked for him, too.

You could try the same approach with agents and managers, but I'd suggest focusing on Producers and Productions Companies. Make it so they have to say yes to at least reading your screenplay. And remember, a succinctly described story idea can get you in the door, but it's your writing that will keep you there.

Chapter 69

Write Short

I may be going against the "write long and cut, cut, cut" flow, but here's the way I make sure that I don't have so many "babies" to kill in my scripts that even after I do edit my work, I'm not saddled with a 160 page monstrosity. Apparently for some of you this is a common problem, this writing long.

Here's a simple fix. Write short instead.

How?

Firstly, write a "silent movie."

Without writing dialogue, compose the screenplay using the briefest descriptions to relay the story. Be descriptive without being novelistic. As stated, it is possible. If you can say the same thing in two words instead of two sentences, do it. Grab the reader's imagination with an economy of words and direct the film in their minds eye. And when I say, "direct the film," I don't mean that literally. Don't place in clunky camera angles, just write descriptively so the reader can imagine the type of angle, or camera shot that would be needed. And please add your personality to the descriptions. Readers want to experience new

Wallflowers Need Not Apply

"voices," it makes their difficult job a little more bearable.

After completing your "silent movie" screenplay, what you'll (hopefully) discover is that you have a solid story in place. It'll basically be an extended outline. Then, and only then, add in the dialogue you need. Again, only the dialogue you need. Don't go all Tarantino on your screenplay at this point. A lot of writers believe that writing a screenplay is all about dialogue. TV writing is mostly about dialogue. Feature film is about story first, dialogue second. Why/how do you think that snappy dialogue works within the context of your favorite movie? The story has you roped in first. Write the story, and then add in only what needs to be said.

"Get into scenes late, get out early." You've probably read that a million times, but there's a lot of validity to it. Example: If it's absolutely necessary to show how your character travels and arrives at their next destination show it, otherwise, cut it.

Be objective and cut any scene that does not advance the story. Yeah, it could possibly be really cool/dramatic/funny shit, but if it's not moving things along it's out of there.

Give these exercises a try on your next draft and you'll probably have a completed screenplay in the 100 page range when all is said and done.

Chapter 70

Freewheeling Into Nothingness

I have to outline my screenplays before I begin writing them.

And you should, too.

I'm not one of those screenwriting savants that can have an idea pop into their head and instantly begin hammering away on the keyboard, cranking out a clean, precise, and readable draft in a matter of hours.

In fact, I don't think screenwriters like that even exist.

Oh, I've spoken with screenwriters (non-produced, of course) who will boast about how they had this great idea come to them the night before in a dream, and now they're working on their third draft. Of course when asked if I can read this treasure, the answer is always the same, "Let me polish it up first." Sure…

If you're jumping right into writing your screenplays based on the first story thoughts that pop into your head, I'd bet the farm that your screenplay is a meandering mess. In fact, I say that the folks who don't outline probably have a box full of 25 page

Wallflowers Need Not Apply

long "first drafts" that they've abandoned because the stories fell apart and they don't know how to fix them because they didn't outline.

Mapping an intriguing and compelling story takes time. It takes a while to create the characters and the world they reside in. Sure, there are going to be times when you'll meander within your story after you create an outline. But the outline (like a map) will always keep you on track so you can arrive at your destination.

Yeah, yeah, I've heard the rumblings about how a few famous screenwriters' have completed drafts on cocktail napkins et al. Great "marketing" hook to lure folks into the theaters, but not believable. They had to outline at some point in the writing process, even if it was outlining after cranking out that first shitty draft. They may have a running mental outline going, but they're outlining.

Maybe – MAYBE – if you're writing a novel you can approach your pages in this freewheeling fashion (Hello Mr. King!), but I don't think that even the above average screenwriter can crank out a saleable screenplay while free writing.

I say it can't be done, so outline!

Chapter 71

Yo, Grammar Nerds

Being grammatically correct throughout your entire written screenplay can be, in two words – fucking boring. Grammatical correctness can take the sharp edges off of your creativity. If all of your characters speak only grammatically correct English, your characters are probably not going to jump off the page. The characters will lack personality, be one-dimensional, and shitty.

If your descriptions are all written in perfect English, they will suck as well. If you read professional screenplays you'll quickly notice what I'm typing about. Fragmented sentences rule the day in screenwriting-dom. Read several professional screenplays and you'll see this for yourself. A good screenwriter twists and turns descriptive phrases for maximum effect.

Of course, you should check your manuscripts for spelling errors. Just don't become handcuffed by proper written language rules when penning your screenplays. Sure, your reader may notice it, but the viewing audience won't if you misuse a semicolon. You can't really film proper semicolon use. And if you're kicking ass with your story, and execution, that reader won't give a shit

Wallflowers Need Not Apply

about any errant semicolons, commas or whatever.

You should try to bend those language rules whenever possible. This all harkens back to your unique "voice."

A Producer will always take a creative and kick-ass screenplay over a grammatically correct and boring one any day of the week.

Dudes, those Grammar Nerds really know how to harsh a screenwriter's creative buzz, man.

Chapter 72

There's No Denying It

Have you ever had your screenwriting ass handed to you?

I did, just now, in fact…

I thought my latest draft was the pinnacle of international screenwriting ability, the shining light of craftsmanship for all other screenplays to be judged by. A screenplay that every demographic would clamor for. A draft that would make the masses dig deep into their pockets for the chance to experience in theaters worldwide. They'd line up in droves, and be amazed by my crafty screenwriting craftsmanship.

Then the Producer read it…

He thought my latest version sucked. He didn't use that specific word, but "suck" was definitely implied.

Turns out, I don't know anything about screenwriting. Nothing. Nada. Zilch. All those years of toiling over blank pages, the carpal tunnel pain, all the networking, the money and time that went into self-educating, and yes, the entirety of the ass kissing

Wallflowers Need Not Apply

I had to do just to get to this point.

It's all for naught.

You know what I'm going do?

Yep, I think I'm going to do it…It is time…

Finally, there's no denying it now.

Especially after all the years of getting eye-rolls from family and friends who've been "supportive" but secretly wonder what in the hell I'm doing seemingly wasting my time on this screenwriting shit.

I know it's a drastic step, but it's time for desperate measures!

What I'm going to do is this…

I'm going to keep writing.

Chapter 73

End At The Ending

I'm glad that you put up with my sometimes repetitive (but important) bullshit and took the time to read the book. Like any decent coach I try to hammer certain points home over and over again. You have to continually learn the basics until those skills are ingrained in every fiber of your screenwriter's being. My comments throughout this book have been directed toward myself as much as they were to you. We all need a kick in the ass from time to time.

Hopefully I was able to entertain while conveying the serious nature of taking a screenwriting career seriously. That is if you are, indeed, serious about making it in the film business.

Write to the best of your ability and creativity. And then write some more - much, much more. Get all the shitty words out of your brain, through your fingertips, and onto the page. The sooner you do that, the quicker you could be writing professionally. I wrote 9 feature-length screenplays before I made a dime at this. It may take you fewer or you may finally get paid after your twentieth screenplay. The reality of this business is that you may

Wallflowers Need Not Apply

never have any monetary gains from your writing. But you'll never know if you have the goods or not until you write and complete screenplays and get them out into the world. It's rather simple, really, just not that easy.

To date, I've written in the area of 60 feature-length screenplays, give or take a few. I lost count because I'm the type of writer who moves on once I've done the best I can with what I had been working on.

And I now move onto my next thing.

Index

Index

A

Accounting 77
Afflect 51
A League of Their Own 128
American Idol 62
Amish Country 93
Antagonist 35, 58, 185
Avatar 33

B

Beowulf 86
Blogs 16
Blood Simple 49
Book rights 17, 160
Bridgette Jones 191
Bronson, Chuck 65
Brooks, Albert 163

C

Censorship 58
Character 28, 31, 33, 37, 43, 44, 58, 59, 67, 72, 73, 83, 84, 102, 111, 113, 120, 126–128, 134, 142, 148–149, 163, 168–169, 174, 179, 183, 185, 194–195, 197
Chevy 58
Cinderella 86
City Slickers 129
Coen Brothers 49
Collaboration 53–54

Comedy 64, 95, 126, 128–129, 148–149, 182, 185
Conference 12, 20–21, 44, 64, 99, 138, 165
Contests 174, 179
Cowell, Simon 105

D

Damon 51
Dialogue 24, 31, 52, 67, 72–73, 111–113, 122, 124, 149, 153, 170, 171, 193–194
Disney 109
Drama 28, 37, 77, 95, 126, 149, 170, 174, 182, 194
Dreamworks 163
Dr. Phil 132

E

Executives 31, 35–36, 42, 74–75, 99, 101–103, 118, 132
Exposition 31, 129

F

Fey, Tina 26
Fight Club 135
Film festival 11–12, 42, 44, 64, 89, 151
Final Draft 15, 113
FTC 50

G

Ganz, Lowell 128
Genre 41, 89, 96, 97
Glengarry Glen Ross 106

H

Hanging orphans 122
Hobby 23, 52, 61, 157
Hollywood Creative Directory 89, 190
Horror 95, 191

I

In and Out Burger 139
Indie filmmaking 47, 74, 138–140, 143, 157–158, 181
Internet Movie Database (IMDB) 9, 89, 190

J

Jackson, Peter 38

K

King Kong 38
Kings Speech, The 142

L

Lemon chicken 23
Library of Congress 144
Little Miss Sunshine 142
Log line 78, 89, 101, 105, 135, 181

M

Mamet, David 106
Mandel, Babaloo 128
Marketing 23, 56, 77, 88, 97, 134, 142–143, 188, 191–192, 196
McKee 174
McMansion 78
McNugget 174

Mies Van Der Rohe 30
Movie Magic 14, 113
Muse, The 163
My Big Fat Greek Wedding 142

N

Networking 12, 20–21, 56, 99, 101, 109, 131, 163–165, 177, 191, 199
New York Times 17, 160
NFL 158
Nicholl Fellowship 179
Night Shift 128
Novel 17, 40, 56–57, 143, 148, 155, 174, 193, 196

O

Old Style beer 84
Option 10, 17, 30, 70, 99, 130, 145, 160–161, 181
Outlining 29

P

Page to minute ratio 17
Panel discussion 11
Parenthetical 113
Parenthood 128
Period pieces 155
Pete's Coffee 59
Pitch 42–43, 56, 64, 75, 99, 101–103, 106, 141, 162, 190
Pitt, Brad 135
Pocahontas 33
Producer 14, 17–18, 26, 30, 35–36, 41–45, 47–49, 56–57, 60, 74–75, 82, 86–88, 101–106, 114, 117, 132, 136–137, 140–141,

142–145, 151, 154, 156, 166, 173, 191–193, 197
Production Company 48–49, 56, 61, 70, 78–79, 90, 99, 116–117, 141, 155, 161, 165, 191–193
Protagonist 37, 66, 110, 183, 185

R

Rewriting 27, 72, 81, 124, 146, 168, 171

S

Sale 31, 35, 40, 90, 97, 102, 126, 132, 135, 143, 155, 190, 196
Screenwriter's salary 16
Screenwriting experts 10, 20, 188
Script Consulting 77, 138, 177
Self-published 18
Smith, John 33
Sold 10, 23, 40, 81, 138, 143, 145, 175
Specs 12, 16–17, 30, 59–63, 70, 78, 86, 95, 97–98, 105–106, 134, 142–145, 155–156, 168, 181
Spielberg, Steven 163
Stanford University 113
Starbuck's 59–60, 84
Star Wars 33
Studio 47, 56, 59, 59–60, 143, 155
Swiffered floors 116

T

Tarantino, Quentin 193

U

USC Film School 55

V

Vlad the Impaler 86
Voice 14, 30–31, 148–149, 174–175, 179, 185, 193, 197

W

Wagner, Paula 172
Wilshire Boulevard 42
World War I 33
Writers Guild of America (WGA) 16–17, 110, 143–144
Writing groups 151

About the Author

JOHN RUSSELL is the pen name of a screenwriter with nearly 20 years of professional experience. He wrote this under a pen name for the simple fact that he wants to continue writing screenplays. "Hollywood" has a way of unofficially disowning those who write books that provide professional advice to novices. Not a good enough reason for you? Okay, think hard about your favorite "book-writing-screenplay-experts" and all the movies they've had hit the theaters in recent years. Go ahead and check Imdb. Couldn't find too many, could you? Now you know why John uses a pseudonym.